# Managing Financial Information

## 2nd edition

David Davies

David Davies, now retired, was a former principal lecturer in financial management at the University of Portsmouth. A qualified accountant with a Masters' degree in Management from Henley Management College, he spent 17 years in the private and public sectors with GEC, Thomas de la Rue, IBM and several local authorities. He has lectured on DPM, MBA, DMS and undergraduate courses, as well as undertaking consultancy work.

The CIPD would like to thank the following members of the CIPD Publishing Editorial Board for their help and advice:

- Pauline Dibben, Middlesex University Business School
- Edwina Hollings, Staffordshire University Business School
- Caroline Hook, Huddersfield University Business School
- Vincenza Priola, Wolverhampton Business School
- John Sinclair, Napier University Business School.

# Managing Financial Information

## 2nd edition

## David Davies

Chartered Institute of Personnel and Development

Published by the Chartered Institute of Personnel and Development, 151 The Broadway, London, SW19 1JQ

This edition published 2005

First edition published 1999

Reprinted 2000, 2001, 2002, 2003 (twice), 2004

Typeset by Curran Publishing Services Ltd, Norwich

Printed in Great Britain by The Cromwell Press, Trowbridge, Wiltshire

*British Library Cataloguing in Publication Data*

A catalogue of this publication is available from the British Library

ISBN 1-84398-003-7

Chartered Institute of Personnel and Development, 151 The Broadway, London, SW19 1JQ
Tel: 020 8612 6200
E-mail: cipd@cipd.co.uk    Website: www.cipd.co.uk
Incorporated by Royal Charter.    Registered Charity No. 1079797

# Contents

**Contents**

# List of figures

# Foreword

This latest edition of *Managing Financial Information* has been prepared specifically to meet the new leadership and management standards of the core management module 'Managing Information for Competitive Advantage'.

The updating includes two new chapters: Introduction to management accounting, and Budgets and human behaviour.

As well as a thorough treatment of the important financial and accounting models, this edition also shows how the theory relates to human resource management systems and practice. This balanced approach allows the student to meet the CIPD requirements of the thinking performer: to be able to make convincing and sophisticated decisions in complex and unpredictable situations, and to be aware of the limitations of concept and theory in relation to problem complexity.

This book must be viewed as essential reading not only for all those who aspire to pass the CIPD module 'Managing Information for Competitive Advantage' but for anyone who wants to become an effective manager and problem solver.

David Allen
CIPD Chief Examiner for
Managing Information for
Competitive Advantage.

# Financial Accounting, Financial Management and Human Resources Practitioners

# PART 1

# Introduction

## CHAPTER 1

Organisations require many resources to enable them to operate successfully in an environment that is competitive and often openly hostile. In the private sector organisational success can be measured in different ways, including the organisation's ability to make profits, generate cash, capture market share or provide a service more effectively than its competitors. The public sector has often found difficulty in justifying the work that it undertakes on the grounds that there is 'no profit motive'. This has dramatically changed in recent years, with value-for-money audits, the need for direct-works organisations to compete in the open market for contracts, and the application of compulsory competitive tendering to all parts of the organisation. Such was the enthusiasm with which this was followed that there was some concern that the public sector would disappear entirely.

In looking at the financial information systems available to help organisations in decision-making, planning and control, however, it is impossible to ignore the fact that there is a legal framework within which they must operate, irrespective of whether they are in the public or the private sector. There are constraints relating to terms and conditions of employment, unfair dismissal and equal opportunities, all of which generally come under the auspices of the human resources manager, as do disciplinary and grievance procedures. The purpose of this introduction is to show a little of the legal framework, but company law is an extremely important area: more detailed coverage is to be found in the books that make up CIPD's Legal Essentials series.

## THE PRIVATE SECTOR

This contains the following three types of business organisation.

### Sole trader

This type of organisation, as the name implies, consists of a single individual who takes full responsibility for all the work that is undertaken. If things go well, and the business is successful, all the profits can be taken and used as the proprietor chooses. On the other hand, if things go badly, and losses are incurred, all his or her personal effects, including the family home, can be called upon to repay creditors.

The sole trader can commence business at any time, with few formalities. It is however, usual to register for value added tax (VAT), and to obtain any necessary planning permission. If the owner wishes to use a company name that differs from his or her own name then the Business Names Act 1985, has to be complied with. The business ceases with the death or retirement of the owner.

## Partnerships

A partnership consists of two or more people who agree to carry on a business, sharing profits and losses in proportions that are the subject of discussion between them. The partnership agreement may be purely verbal, but is usually in writing. It sets out the way in which profits and losses are to be shared as well as any salaries that are to be received by the partners. A partnership, like a sole trader, can start business at any time with few formalities other than the necessity of obtaining any necessary planning permission, registering for VAT, and complying with the Business Names Act 1985.

The death of a partner can lead to the dissolution of the partnership, but more usually the agreement will provide for the business to continue under the remaining partner(s). It will be necessary for the continuing partner(s) to buy out the share of the deceased, with consequent problems in raising finance. The basic rules that apply to a partnership are found in the Partnership Act 1890, which, together with the general law of the land, governs its activities.

## Companies

There are two types of company, the limited (LTD), which is not allowed to offer its shares to the general public, and the public limited company (PLC), whose shares are offered to the public at large through the medium of the Stock Exchange. Both consist of two or more people incorporated as a registered company, who become its shareholders, and appoint directors to manage the company and act as its agents. The shareholders must also appoint a company secretary. The company cannot commence business until the formalities have been completed. They include a certificate of incorporation from the Registrar of Companies, compliance with the Companies Act 1985, and the Business Names Act 1985, and usually registration for VAT.

The company has a separate legal entity from the owners, and its existence is unaffected by the death or retirement of any of them. On the other hand, it has a far more complex legal environment in which to operate than either the sole trader or the partnership. It has an obligation to file accounts annually, together with the Directors' and Auditors' reports. These items are retained by the Registrar of Companies and are available for inspection on request from Companies House. Annual general meetings must be held, so that shareholders are kept informed of corporate activities and, in addition, the Articles and Memorandum of Association set out the limits of the company's activities in pursuance of its trade.

# THE PUBLIC SECTOR

This contains three types of organisation: the commercial public organisation, the social services organisation, and the local government organisation.

## Commercial public corporations

These receive their authority and constraints from the government, and are run on commercial lines under the control of a minister.

## Social service organisations

These also receive their authority from the government, on whose behalf they run a social service, such as the Health and Safety Executive.

The commercial public corporations and social service organisations each have a separate legal entity, and their objects and powers are contained in the Act of Parliament that created them.

## Local authorities

These derive their powers and limitations from the Acts of Parliament and charters that created them. They have a great many obligatory duties and enormous permissive powers, but they must take great care that they do nothing that is *ultra vires* (outside their powers), for if they do they have to pay for the consequences. They are independent within the powers authorised by the central government.

The public sector organisations employ large numbers of people, so that the death or retirement of an individual has no effect on their existence. They have a statutory duty to account for the manner in which they discharge their responsibilities, and must appoint auditors to report on the activities of the period under review. Accounts have to be prepared for the central government, which are open to inspection by the general public. In recent years the government's concern to obtain value for money has put local authorities under close public scrutiny. As a result, they are considered to have become more efficient.

The conditions under which such concerns operate are complex, and all are restricted in what they are legally entitled to do. This makes it essential for them to take legal advice when they are established, to help ensure that the purpose for which they have been set up is a legitimate one. The human resources manager has an important role in ensuring that the conditions of employment are fully met. This will help ensure that the organisations enjoy the confidence of the general public that they serve.

The current climate confirms that the public and private sectors have to compete for scarce resources to enable them to operate at all, and if they are to grow they have to be seen to be performing successfully in order to attract those resources. Both sectors need people, materials, machinery, equipment, buildings, money and information. Although each of these is important, this book is mostly concerned with how the human resources manager obtains and uses financial resources for the benefit of the organisation. The decisions of such managers and others are translated into the international language of money, which gives a common understanding of plans and enables the performance of organisations, and individuals within those organisations, to be monitored and controlled. This cannot be achieved, however, without frequent and accurate financial information in the right form reaching the right people at the right time to enable them to make good use of it. Human resources managers among many others, need to keep a close eye on the cash position. The way in which money moves through a manufacturing concern may be illustrated by the way in which water flows through a series of reservoirs and pipes (Figure 1).

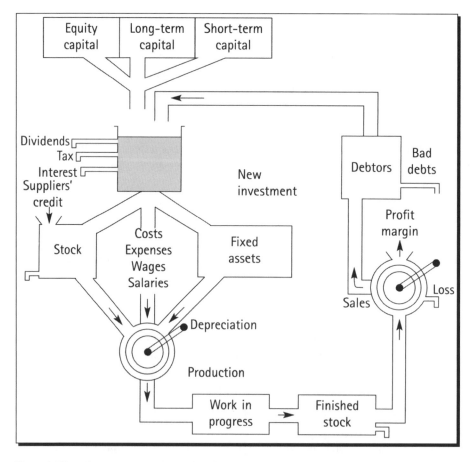

**Figure 1** *Where the money goes in a manufacturing concern*

The reservoirs of inventory, capital, work in progress, finished goods and debtors represent traps in which money may build up. If they are allowed to become too large, cash-flow problems will result. The management information system should therefore highlight these potential problems, so that management is made aware of them early enough for remedial action to be taken to correct the situation before it becomes serious. Good management practice, which is represented by the pumps, supported by useful, timely information, ensures that any delays which occur are kept to an absolute minimum. The human resources manager can contribute to a cash flow by helping to ensure that an efficient credit controller is appointed, thus helping to keep debtors to a reasonable level.

The public sector is under exactly the same pressures to ensure that the best possible use is made of the people, money and other resources available to it, and that no hold-ups occur in the efficient running of the organisation. Both sectors are responsible for planning their activities and controlling actions as they take place, so that targets are met and the instructions of management carried out. Human resources managers ensure that an organisation's goals are achieved through its people. Failure to perform to the required standard leads to job losses and possibly the demise of the organisation. Sources of finance may show a different emphasis, with much of the public-sector money coming from the business rate, council tax and government grants, whilst the private sector is responsible for obtaining its resources direct from the public. They both provide goods and services with the monies obtained, and compete in the provision of such services as old people's and children's homes, refuse collection and housing maintenance, as well as housing itself.

In view of this commonality, Figure 2 is appropriate to both the non-manufacturing private sector and the non-manufacturing public sector of the economy. We can see that the control of levels of stock/inventory and debtors is extremely important for all organisations. The ways in which this control may be achieved are discussed later in the book, but the efficiency of the organisation depends on the correct information being available in the right place, at the right time, and then being promptly acted upon by correctly trained people.

This book has been written to give human resource practitioners a clear understanding of the processes outlined above, and of the role of financial and management accounts and how they may be employed to clarify the financial performance of organisations and aid decision-making.

The first part of this book explores the role of financial accounting and financial management, with particular reference to their application to human resource practitioners. Financial accounting was developed to help business people ensure that their money and resources were not being misappropriated by those who were being employed to act on their behalf. The financial accounts consist of the balance sheet,

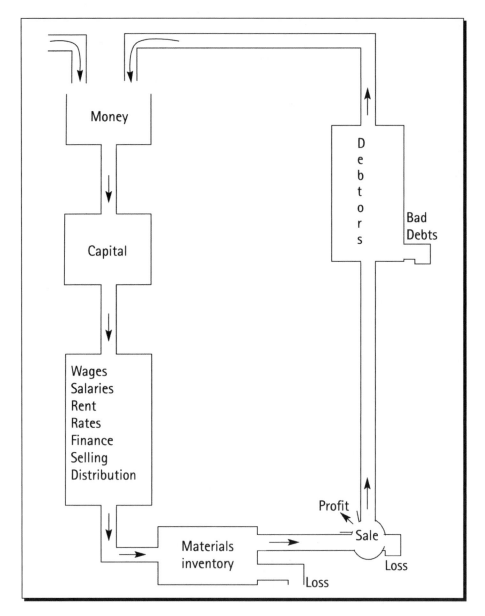

**Figure 2** *Where the money goes in a non-manufacturing organisation*

which shows the financial position of the organisation at a particular date, the trading and profit and loss account, which shows whether a profit has been made or a loss incurred as the result of a period of trading, and the manufacturing account, which shows how much the goods made have cost. The balance sheet and these accounts, together with their application to personnel, will be considered in Chapters 4, 5 and 6.

Financial management developed in the nineteenth and twentieth centuries as organisations became more complex and it became necessary to have information that aided decision-making as well as providing proof of stewardship. This led to the use of ratios which helped management ensure that the organisation for which they were responsible was meeting its targets. If it was demonstrated that the targets were not being met, reasons could be ascertained and remedial action taken before the situation became critical. These ratios and their application to human resources will be examined in Chapters 7 and 8.

Part II examines management accounting and its utility to human resources practitioners through: absorption costing, which allocates costs and illustrates the link between financial and management accounts; marginal costing, which considers costs that are relevant to specific decisions; standard costing, which sets an expected cost and compares it with the actual cost. Finally, the whole process of planning and control is fully explored. These topics are covered in Chapters 9 to 17 and the book has been set out in a logical sequence that facilitates learning, supported by practical examples to help understanding.

# The Finance Function and the Human Resources Manager

## CHAPTER 2

## OBJECTIVE

At the end of this chapter the student will understand the role of the finance function and its links with the human resources department. The management standards that this chapter will help to develop are to 'manage financial resources to achieve goals and objectives through the budgetary planning and control process'.

It is important for the human resources manager to understand the role of the finance function in an organisation, since a proportion of the finances obtained will be required by that department. The financial manager is responsible for obtaining financial resources as cheaply as possible and ensuring that they are effectively employed by the organisation. This is more likely to be achieved in the human resources department if the human resources manager and the financial manager work closely together towards a common goal. There are three main decisions that have to be made by the financial manager, and they are discussed in turn.

### The financing decision

This is the first major decision of the organisation. What sources are to be used to obtain finance and in what proportions? In the private sector, the amount that can be raised by the issue of shares or by borrowing is limited by the Articles and Memorandum of Association. Nonetheless, the proportions in which the money is raised through the issues of shares or in other ways has an impact on the cost of the resources as well as on the public's perception of the firm. Companies that borrow a high proportion of their financial resources as opposed to issuing shares are said to be highly geared or leveraged, and are perceived to be high-risk concerns. The most popular source of finance for existing companies in the private sector is internally generated funds or retained profits.

The ways in which organisations in the public sector can obtain finance are laid down by statute and they are constrained by the principle of *ultra vires*. This means that certain actions are beyond the powers of these organisations, and sets boundaries within which they must function. Even so the head of the financial department has a good deal of discretion in deciding where borrowed monies should be obtained, although there must obviously be clear public accountability. The monies raised are used first to enable the organisation to continue to operate, and will be allocated to department heads, including human resources, on the basis agreed in the budget.

Second, they can be allocated to capital projects which will be discussed later in the book.

## The investment decision

The second major decision is how the funds that the organisation has obtained should be invested. Here again the private sector has rather more discretion than the public, which has a statutory duty to provide such services as public health and housing. The financial manager, in conjunction with the human resources manager and other members of the management team, has to decide how much should be invested in fixed assets like land and building, plant, machinery and equipment, and how much in current assets like inventory or stock.

## The asset management decision

The financial manager helps to decide how the assets that have been acquired should be managed. It is in the nature of organisations that once fixed assets have been obtained they remain *in situ* for several years. This tends to make managers concentrate their attention in the short term on current asset management (ie stock, debtors and cash)

The management team works to deploy the assets together with the human resources manager responsible for both the normal departmental assets and the most valuable assets that any organisation possesses – its people. We cannot put an inventory value on people, but companies such as Marks & Spencer, which makes special efforts to manage and motivate its staff, invariably see the results coming through on the bottom line in the form of increased profits. Admittedly, there are occasional hiccups as change takes place as is currently being demonstrated. Since the end of 2000 there has been a general slump, some might argue a crash, in the stock market, which means that share prices have fallen sharply and many organisations have gone into liquidation. Marks & Spencer has followed this trend and has been struggling to reassert its prominent market position but, despite its recent loss of profits, it is not in danger of going into liquidation.

## The management information system

The financial manager has another important role to play: he or she operates the financial information system. Most organisations now have a computerised system that shows managers how well they are working to plan. This information is usually produced monthly, although it can be done more frequently, and it is the financial manager's responsibility to ensure that the information is up to date, received on time and is accurate. It is no good informing the human resources manager that the department is £20,000 over budget three months after the end of the year to which the information relates. By then it is too late to take any remedial action.

The human resources, financial and other managers should discuss the information they require in order to run their departments effectively. (Examples of how finance fits into the overall organisational structure in the private sector and in a local authority are shown in Figure 3.) Once what is required is known, the timing and detail of the information should be agreed. It is no use for the system to produce a 30-page report if only four pages are being used, not only because it is a waste of paper but more

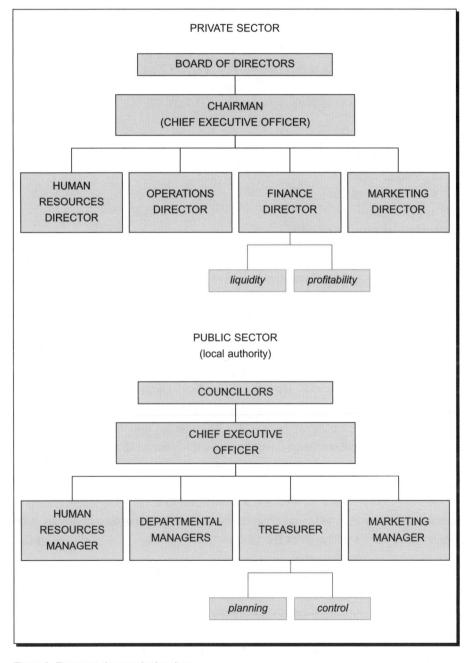

**Figure 3** *Finance on the organisation chart*

importantly because it is an ineffective use of a manager's time to be looking at information that is not relevant to the job in hand.

The financial manager is responsible for raising money as cheaply as possible and using it effectively within the context of the organisation that is being served. In order to achieve this the objective or goal of the organisation must be known so that the context within which the management is operating is clear. We will now look more closely at the sources from which money is obtained and the ways in which it can be employed.

## THE SOURCES AND USES OF CAPITAL

Figure 1 in Chapter 1 demonstrates the three types of finance required by organisations:

- permanent/equity capital
- long-term capital
- short-term capital.

### Permanent equity capital

This is, the money provided for the organisation by its owners, which does not have to be repaid as long as the organisation continues as a going concern.

In the private sector the money provided by the owners is in the form of share capital, and profits that have been retained in the organisation (when it has traded successfully) become reserves. The share capital can be broken down into various types of shares. The ordinary share capital is the equity capital and gives the holder the right to vote on the way in which the organisation should operate. The wishes of the shareholders are carried out by their elected representatives, the board of directors, and each director would normally be expected to hold a large number of ordinary shares in that company. Directors who did not hold a large number of shares would be viewed with suspicion, as it would seem that they had no confidence in the organisation they were running. The company is under no obligation to buy back any of the shares that it has sold, although it may decide to do so. The normal means of recovering money invested in an organisation through the purchase of shares is by selling those shares on the Stock Exchange.

The ordinary shareholders, or equity holders, carry the biggest risk of all those who provide money for an organisation. There is no stated rate of return on their investment, and if the company does not do well they get no dividend. They are the last to receive a return on their investment and the last to be paid in the event of failure, ranking after all the other creditors, secured or unsecured. In the past the ordinary shareholders have found it difficult to influence the decisions of the board of a company, but this has changed and they are having a major impact on appointments and the remuneration of directors. The shareholders' refusal to accept the appointment of Michael Green as chairman of the merged Granada-Carlton was an example of this new-found power, as was the vote against the £23 million pay packet of Jean-Pierre Garnier, chief executive of GlaxoSmithKline. There has also been uproar at BskyB over the proposal to replace the chief executive Tony Ball by Rupert Murdoch's son, James.

There are other shareholders who provide permanent capital. They are called preference shareholders and, as the name implies, they are in a preferential position vis-à-vis the ordinary shareholders with regard to the receipt of dividends and the return of their money should the business fail. In view of this reduced risk, the preference shareholders do not normally have voting rights when major decisions concerning the running of the company are made. Preference shares, like ordinary shares, can be bought and sold through the Stock Exchange.

The purpose of the Stock Exchange is to act as a marketplace and bring together the providers and users of capital. Companies that wish to be listed on the exchange must have a proven record of profitability over a number of years and submit to a thorough investigation by the Stock Exchange before the privilege is granted. Those companies that are listed find their ability to raise permanent capital greatly enhanced, provided market conditions are conducive to the issue of shares.

Companies that wish to raise money through the issue of shares usually use the services of an issuing house, which will give advice on the timing and size of the issue and the price at which the shares should be offered, and will also underwrite such an issue. Press advertisements give details of the issue and invite applications for the purchase of shares. Payment is normally required in more than one instalment or tranche; for example, if the shares were to be sold for £1.50 each, payment might be requested as 50p on application, 50p on first call and 50p on second and final call, so that the shares might not be fully paid for until three or four years after they had been received. Individuals wishing to sell shares they already own would also use the Stock Exchange, but they would employ the services of a stockbroker rather than an issuing house.

The permanent capital having been raised, it is the responsibility of the organisation's management to ensure that it is put to good use immediately. The purpose for which it was raised would have been stated at the time the public was invited to invest, and business should be started as quickly as possible in order to avoid criticism that might make it difficult to raise money in the future.

Permanent capital is needed to build or expand an organisation, through the purchase of fixed assets, such as plant and machinery, land and buildings, fixtures and fittings, or through the purchase of another company. On the other hand, it might be used to increase the working capital, which is what enables an undertaking to keep running until it earns some more money from its operations, and out of which all its running expenses are met.

Working capital is tied up in inventory, debtors and the bank, and lack of it severely restricts an organisation's ability to operate successfully. The injection of fresh working capital can lead to increased operating levels, giving greater profitability and hence additional retained profits.

## Long-term capital

Long-term capital consists of borrowed monies which will remain in the company for five or more years, and sometimes carries the option of being converted into ordinary share capital at the discretion of the lender. Normally, long-term loans are secured by a charge on the fixed assets of the borrowing concern, so that if things do not go well the lenders are certain of recovering their money through the sale of the fixed assets if necessary. Only the most successful organisations, like Tesco or BP, are able to raise loans that are not secured on their fixed assets, as lenders feel that their money is safe with them and that the conditions on which it was lent will be honoured in full.

Loans may be raised through the stock market, particularly if they are to be convertible loans, but more usually the services of the other institutions of the City of London would be employed. It may be possible to raise money through one of the clearing banks, such as Barclays, LloydsTSB, HSBC or NatWest, but it should be remembered that they are not normally providers of venture capital and look for absolute security in their lending. Recent events have demonstrated, however, that they are not infallible where organisations have failed and their debts have had to be written off.

More likely sources of long-term capital are the merchant banks, which specialize rather more in the provision of venture capital, but would still take an extremely close look at the organisation's prospects and any available security before lending money. 3i (Investors in Industry) are the biggest suppliers of venture capital in the United Kingdom.

The pension funds are always looking for good investment opportunities, but they too prefer safe investments, both from the point of view of income – that is, the dividend received – and from that of capital growth – the increase in the value of the investment. They are prohibited from lending money. The Business Expansion Scheme also exists to bring together organisations that require capital and those prepared to provide it, facilitated by special tax provisions to attract the providers of capital. This now seems to be nearing the end of its useful life.

These are the main providers of long-term capital, but there are others, and the list is by no means comprehensive. It should be remembered that, wherever the capital is obtained, the lender will need to be assured of its safety. The less security there is, the higher will be the charge for the money, if it can be obtained at all. A secured loan may be obtained at 5 per cent but an unsecured loan could cost as much as 13 per cent, and to make that worth while the user should ensure that at least 16 per cent is being earned – a requirement beyond most organisations.

Borrowed money can be used either externally or internally: externally to repay previous borrowings or, within the organisation, to enable it to operate more effectively. Whatever is done must be perceived as being to the benefit of the borrowing organisation, otherwise it will prove both difficult and expensive to raise further funds in the future.

## Short-term capital

Short-term capital, in the form of loans that have to be repaid within five years, can be raised from the same sources as long-term capital and on broadly similar terms, although there will be differences in the rate of interest charged. The expertise of the financial management function is tested when borrowing money, in that it is its job to obtain the best possible terms, whilst the lenders will be endeavouring to achieve the same for themselves. When interest rates are high the lenders will want to lend for as long as possible and at a fixed rate of interest, while the borrower will want the loan to be for as short term as possible and at a variable rate of interest, in the expectation that it will quickly fall. Interest rates are currently (2005/6) at a historically low level and are not expected to increase by much if at all.

The amount of borrowing and the terms on which money is lent will be decided largely by the City's view of the organisation and its present capital structure: that is to say, the proportion of borrowed money in relation to that belonging to the owners. Where the proportion of borrowing is large, the organisation is said to be 'highly geared' and it may be extremely difficult to borrow any further money.

The question of gearing is complex but we can say that the more highly geared an organisation is, the greater the risk a prospective lender is taking and the higher the return that will be expected. A general rule with respect to the use of borrowed monies is that you do not borrow short to invest long. This means that short-term borrowing should not be invested in fixed assets, because if it were, it might be necessary to sell the fixed assets when the time came to repay the loan. Generally, short-term borrowing should be employed in short-term investment, so that if necessary the money can be obtained easily when it has to be repaid.

These principles apply to both the private and the public sectors when they wish to raise money through the marketplace, except that local authorities are generally seen as more secure places in which to invest money. Nonetheless, they still have to compete in terms of interest

The proportion of funds that is obtained directly through the institutions of the City of London varies between the public and private sectors, in that in local government a large proportion of the money is obtained through the council tax, the business rate, and government grants. Figure 4 shows how Portsmouth City Council was funded in 2003/4

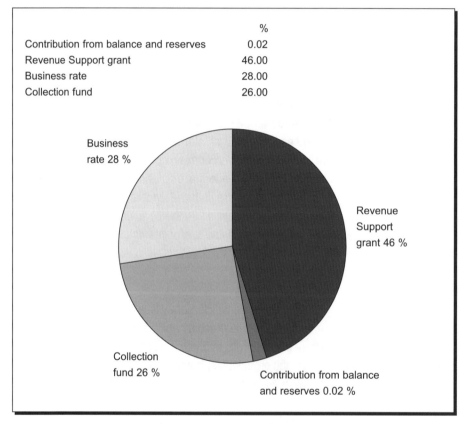

| | % |
|---|---|
| Contribution from balance and reserves | 0.02 |
| Revenue Support grant | 46.00 |
| Business rate | 28.00 |
| Collection fund | 26.00 |

**Figure 4** *Portsmouth City Council funding*

This chapter has given you an insight to the role of the finance function and helped demonstrate its links with human resources.

## SELF-TEST QUESTIONS

1. What is share capital?
2. What is a dividend?
3. What is inventory or stock?
4. What are the three major decisions that have to be made by the financial manager?
5. What is a fixed asset?
6. What is short-term capital and how can it be obtained?

## Work-based assignment

Ascertain the sources from which your organisation obtains its financial resources and the basis on which they are allocated to the human resources department.

# The Human Resources Manager and Management Information Systems

## OBJECTIVE

At the end of this chapter the student will understand financial information systems and their use to the human resources manager. The standards this chapter will help to develop are 'managing financial resources to achieve goals and objectives through the budgetary planning and control process and the interpretation of information from key financial statements'.

The environment in which organisations operate is so complex that it would be impossible for them to survive without detailed planning, monitoring and the use of information from a great variety of sources. It follows, therefore, that organisations must set up information systems that are helpful to management in running the operations for which they are responsible. This chapter looks at some of the financial information systems that are available to the human resources manager: they will be discussed in greater detail later in the book.

In planning it is necessary to have information, since no plan can be devised in a vacuum. The bulk of this information in most organisations is derived from actions that have taken place in the past. Management looks at what has been happening over the last five years, with particular emphasis on the last year. Then, with the aid of economic forecasts and reports from their own sources, they attempt to decide what will happen to the organisation over the next five or six years. It is extremely unlikely that any of these forecasts will be 100 per cent accurate even for the next year, but there is no doubt that the more information that is available the more accurate the forecast is likely to be.

Organisations that are new and making their forecasts for the first time are at something of a disadvantage in that they have no first-hand experience on which to draw. This does not mean that they should not attempt to plan – indeed, it is absolutely essential that they do, because organisations that do not plan fail. The lack of first-hand experience is a drawback, but there are normally other undertakings operating in the same field and much information can be obtained about them through publications such as Dunn and Bradstreet's *Key British enterprises*, as well as by spending money on market research. This will enable the new organisation to prepare a fairly well-informed plan of activity at least for the next year, and as those responsible for planning gain experience their plans will improve.

Once the plan has been drawn up, it is essential that it is monitored continuously, so that differences between planned and actual performance can be readily seen, and corrective action taken where it is felt to be necessary. This can be achieved only if the relevant information is available at the right place and at the right time. One of the dangers of high technology is that those responsible for making decisions receive so much information that it is sometimes difficult to 'see the wood for the trees', and important things are overlooked. It is no use telling the sales manager the number of employees in the production department, or the production manager the cost of recruiting a human resources manager, at least from the point of view of their decision-making. Nor is it useful to tell a production manager at the end of August that s/he failed to meet the production target in January, as the information will be too late to be of any use at all. It is here that a good management information system is invaluable to any organisation.

The human resources department has to work within organisational constraints, and the overall plan, but the resources available to it will depend, to some extent, on the personality of the human resources manager. When the budget is being prepared, each departmental manager will bid for the resources required for his or her department. The manager who is perceived to be providing good value for money and has prepared a strong case will, generally speaking, receive a larger share of the available resources than a less well-prepared and informed manager. It is therefore essential for the well-being of the human resources department, as well as for the organisation as a whole, that the human resources manager is fully conversant with the system of budgetary control employed by the undertaking in which he or she is employed.

Having obtained an equitable share of the resources available, it is incumbent upon the human resources manager to demonstrate that the department is providing good value for its investment. In order to achieve this, each item of expenditure must be carefully measured against the best available alternative to demonstrate that expenditure is being incurred because it is needed and not simply because this is the way things have always been done. Methods of developing proposals have to be continually reviewed to see whether it might be better to buy in expertise rather than supply it internally, and it is now becoming more common for human resources departments to offer their training programmes in the open market as a way of obtaining additional income for training and development.

A system of budgeting is illustrated in Figure 5, which demonstrates that there is feedback and control at every stage, and it is essential for the system to produce this information quickly and accurately. The budgetary system is an overall system of planning within an organisation that ends in the master budget. This consists of statements of vital importance to organisational survival: the balance sheet, profit and

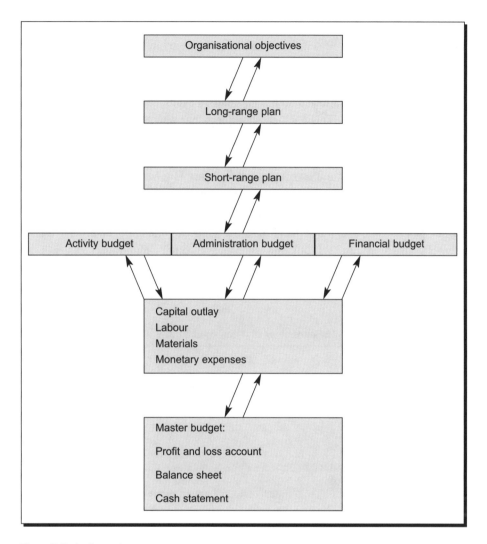

**Figure 5** *Budgeting systems*

loss account, and cash statement, each of which will be discussed in this chapter and analysed in depth later in the book.

The *balance sheet* provides information on the position of an organisation at a given date. It relates only to that date, since the position may vary significantly from day to day, which makes the date on which the balance sheet was prepared extremely important, as are the conventions that have been followed in drawing it up. Traditionally the balance sheet has been employed largely as a historical document, showing the organisation's position at some point in the past and allowing relevant information to be derived from it.

There is no reason, however, why the balance sheet should not be used, as it is more often tending to be, as a planning document, to show what an organisation will look like at some future date. The future position of the undertaking is of greater importance to those who are involved with it than what has happened in the past, although past lessons should never be forgotten.

The balance sheet is a specific sort of information system and its two-sided form is illustrated in Example 1. This balance sheet, together with others, will be discussed in greater detail in Chapter 4, but it can readily be seen that it could be used by the personnel manager to obtain information that might be helpful in counselling staff. The company, 'X Co.' has a liquidity problem. There is a bank overdraft of £10,000 and no cash available at all, which seems to make it very difficult for 'X Co.' to pay its way. This information could be useful, for example, when advising staff on their career plans. This and much more can be deduced when the balance sheet is correctly used in conjunction with ratios, and other information, as will be demonstrated in Chapter 4.

*Example 1*

Balance sheet of 'X Co.' as at 31 July

| | £ | £ | | £ | £ |
|---|---|---|---|---|---|
| Fixed assets | | | Capital | 100,000 | |
| Land and buildings | 180,000 | | Reserves | 90,000 | |
| Plant and machinery | 90,000 | | | | 190,000 |
| Motor vehicles | 25,000 | | | | |
| | | 295,000 | Loans | | 90,000 |
| Current assets | | | Current liabilities | | |
| Stock | 5,000 | | Creditors | 40,000 | |
| Debtors | 50,000 | | Accruals | 20,000 | |
| | | 55,000 | Bank overdraft | 10,000 | |
| | | | | | 70,000 |
| | | 350,000 | | | 350,000 |

The *profit and loss account*, as its name suggests, gives information as to whether or not a business, or part of it, is making a profit or loss. Like the balance sheet, it can be used either as an historical document or as a planning tool. It relates to a period of time, which may be a month, a quarter, a half-year, a year or any other period of time over which the organisation wishes to measure the success or failure of its operations. The information that it provides will be altered by the conventions that have been followed in its preparation, particularly in the treatment of depreciation, research and development, and goodwill.

This account is divided into two parts, the first of which records the cost of the goods that have been sold, and compares it with the selling price to give the gross profit. The second part takes from the gross profit fixed costs like salaries, rates, depreciation, interest charges and stationery, to arrive at the net profit.

The profit and loss account is illustrated in Example 2, but it should be borne in mind that businesses which provide a service do not normally need to calculate a gross profit. The example shows a net profit of £30,000, but we do not yet have sufficient information to know whether that is good or bad; this and other points will be explained in Chapter 5. *Opening inventory* means the stock in hand at the beginning of the period being considered. *Closing inventory* means the stock in hand at the end of that period.

*Example 2*

Trading and profit and loss account of 'X Co.' for the year ending 31 July

|  | £ | £ |
|---|---|---|
| Sales |  | 600,000 |
| *Less* cost of goods sold: |  |  |
| Opening inventory | 10,000 |  |
| *Add* inventory purchased | 360,000 |  |
|  | 370,000 |  |
|  |  |  |
| *Deduct* closing inventory | 50,000 |  |
| Cost of inventory sold |  | 320,000 |
|  |  |  |
| Gross profit |  | 280,000 |
| *Less* expenses: |  |  |
| Wages and salaries | 150,000 |  |
| Selling and distribution | 20,000 |  |
| Heating and lighting | 10,000 |  |
| Depreciation | 30,000 |  |
| Financing charges | 30,000 |  |
| Miscellaneous | 10,000 | 250,000 |
|  |  |  |
| Net profit |  | 30,000 |

The *cash statement* shows the cash position of an organisation, and the balance appears in the balance sheet, either under the current assets as bank/cash in hand or under the current liabilities as bank overdrawn at that date. The statement can be used either for historical reporting purposes or for planning and control, and is commonly utilised in both these ways. The information it contains is of vital importance to the survival of the organisation, as, without money, operations would have to cease. When used as a system of planning and control, the cash statement is referred to as a cash budget and prepared on a daily, weekly, monthly or quarterly basis, and is closely monitored, as described in Chapters 16 and 17.

This is one of the most important financial management information systems, and it is almost impossible to pay too much attention to this aspect of an organisation. Example 3 shows a cash statement which indicates that the major reason for the overdraft of £20,000 is the capital expenditure of £200,000 on fixed assets during the year.

*Example 3*

Cash statement of 'X Co.' for the year ending 31 July

| | £ | £ |
|---|---|---|
| Opening cash in hand/(overdrawn) | | 60,000 |
| Receipts from cash sales | 100,000 | |
| Receipts from credit sales | 400,000 | |
| | | 500,000 |
| | | 560,000 |
| Total cash available | | |
| *Deduct* payments: | | |
| Payments for cash purchases | 160,000 | |
| Payments for credit purchases | 80,000 | |
| Wages and salaries | 40,000 | |
| Selling and distribution costs | 40,000 | |
| Heating and lighting | 20,000 | |
| Financing charges | 30,000 | |
| Miscellaneous costs | 10,000 | |
| Fixed assets purchased | 200,000 | |
| | | 580,000 |
| Cash in hand/(overdrawn) | | (20,000) |

The human resources manager will be responsible for preparing the cash budget and monitoring the cash statement of his or her department. This control will normally take place on a daily basis as it is essential for the human resources manager (and indeed the whole organisation) to be constantly aware of the cash position and, where necessary, to react with the utmost speed. Many chief executives now insist that any surpluses are invested in the overnight market in order to make money.

This chapter has introduced you to the planning system and its links to human resources. In particular the budgetary system, the balance sheet, the income statement or profit and loss account and the cash statement have been illustrated, and their use to human resources stated.

## SELF-TEST QUESTIONS

1. What is meant by a sole trader?
2. How does a limited company differ from a public limited company?
3. What is the public sector?
4. What is the private sector?
5. What is meant by a management information system?
6. How is the budget useful to the human resources manager?
7. Why is it important to monitor the cash position?

## Work-based assignment

Obtain your organisation's budget and final accounts, and discuss with your human resources manager the ways in which the information might be used.

# The Balance Sheet and the Human Resources Manager

## OBJECTIVE

At the end of this chapter the reader will understand the structure of the balance sheet and its use in providing information to the human resources manager. The standard that this chapter will help to develop is 'interpreting information from key financial statements'.

The balance sheet is a statement that shows the position of the organisation at a specific date, and like all statements its accuracy is dependent on the information system employed to compile it. If the information on which it is based is inaccurate, the balance sheet will be inaccurate. This illustrates the central role of a good management information system in the effective running of an organisation. In drawing up a balance sheet it is necessary to follow accounting conventions, which will be explored as we work through some illustrations.

*Example 4*

Business balance sheet as at day 1

| Uses: | £ | Sources: | £ |
|---|---|---|---|
| Bank | £240,000 | Capital | £240,000 |

An entrepreneur has £240,000 with which to start a business and pays it into the business's bank account. The balance sheet would be as shown in Example 4. It shows that £240,000 has been put into the business by the owner and that at the time of the balance sheet it was all in the bank. Any resource put into a business by the owner(s) becomes part of the capital, and all sources of finance are shown on the right-hand side of the two-sided balance sheet. The uses of finance, including money in the bank, are shown on the left-hand side. Every balance sheet uses these principles, and if they are broken down item by item a great deal of the confusion that often surrounds them can readily be overcome.

*Example 5*

Business balance sheet as at day 2

| Uses: | £ | Sources: | £ |
|---|---|---|---|
| Premises | £100,000 | Capital | £240,000 |
| Bank | £140,000 | | |
| | £240,000 | | £240,000 |

Premises are required for the business, and enquiries lead to the purchase of a small lock-up shop for £100,000 on day 2. The shop is paid for and the balance sheet on that day is shown in Example 5. No new resources have been put into the business by the owner, nor have any been withdrawn, which leaves the capital unchanged; and, as no other resources have been provided, there is no change on the 'sources' side of the balance sheet. On the 'uses' side the money has been taken from the bank and invested in the premises, as reflected in the new balance sheet.

*Example 6*

### Business balance sheet as at day 3

| Uses: | £ | Sources: | £ |
|---|---|---|---|
| Premises | £100,000 | Capital | £240,000 |
| Inventory/stock | £2,000 | | |
| Bank | £138,000 | | |
| | £240,000 | | £240,000 |

The premises having been obtained, the business now requires inventory to sell in order to start trading. £2,000 of goods are purchased for cash on day 3. This transaction will be shown in the balance sheet as in Example 6. The sources side of the balance sheet remains unchanged but there has been a further change of use. £2,000 has been taken from the bank to purchase inventory, which is also referred to as stock, consisting of items held by the business for resale in order to earn a profit.

*Example 7*

### Business balance sheet as at day 6

| Uses: | £ | Sources: | £ |
|---|---|---|---|
| Premises | £100,000 | Capital | £240,000 |
| Inventory/stock | £1,800 | | |
| Bank | £138,200 | | |
| | £240,000 | | £240,000 |

Inventory that cost £200 is sold for £200 on day 6 to attract people into the shop. The balance sheet will then be as shown in Example 7. Once again the sources side of the balance sheet remains unchanged but the inventory is reduced by the £200 that has been sold and the bank increased by the £200 that has been received from the sale.

*Example 8*

Business balance sheet as at day 8

| Uses: | £ | Sources: | £ |
|---|---|---|---|
| Premises | £100,000 | Capital | £240,000 |
| Inventory/stock | £200 | Reserves | |
| Bank | £141,400 | Retained profit | £1,600 |
| | £241,600 | | £241,600 |

On day 8 the business is really ready for action, and inventory that cost £1,600 is sold for £3,200 cash. The resulting balance sheet is shown in Example 8. The sources side of the balance sheet is increased by the profit on the sale of £1,600, which is shown under the reserves. This is balanced by the reduction in inventory of £1,600 and the increased bank balance of £3,200, which illustrates the fact that all the resources a business receives must be accounted for, whatever their nature, and explains why the balance sheet should always balance. The premises remain unchanged at £100,000.

*Example 9*

Business balance sheet as at day 9

| Uses: | £ | Sources: | £ |
|---|---|---|---|
| Premises | £100,000 | Capital | £240,000 |
| Inventory/stock | £6,200 | Reserves | |
| | | Retained profit | £1,600 |
| Bank | £137,400 | Creditor | £2,000 |
| | £243,600 | | £243,600 |

The business is now in full stride and on day 9 further inventory is purchased for £6,000, of which £4,000 is in cash and £2,000 is credit (Example 9). A new item appears on the sources side of the balance sheet, called creditor, of £2,000. Creditors are people who are owed money by the business for goods or services they have provided. This item is balanced by an increase of £6,000 in the inventory and a reduction in the bank balance of £4,000; no other changes take place in the balance sheet. It is interesting to note that the reserves are £1,600 but the bank balance is £137,400. Reserves do not normally equal cash.

Business is booming. To encourage it, credit is offered to reliable customers, and on day 10 inventory that cost £3,600 is sold for £7,200. The sales consist of £1,200 for cash and £6,000 on credit. The balance sheet is shown in Example 10. The capital and creditor on the sources side remain unchanged, whilst the reserves are increased by

*Example 10*

Business balance sheet as at day 10

| Uses: | £ | Sources: | £ |
|---|---|---|---|
| Premises | £100,000 | Capital | £240,000 |
| Inventory/stock | £2,600 | Reserves | |
| Debtors | £6,000 | Retained profit | £5,200 |
| Bank | £138,600 | Creditor | £2,000 |
| | £247,200 | | £247,200 |

the profit of £3,600 to £5,200, although the bank balance is £138,600. Reserves do not represent cash. On the uses side, inventory is reduced by the £3,600 that has been sold, to £2,600, the bank balance is increased by the £1,200 received from the sale, to £138,600, and debtors of £6,000 for the credit sales appear. People who owe money to the business for goods or services received are called debtors.

*Example 11*

Business balance sheet as at day 11

| Uses: | £ | Sources: | £ |
|---|---|---|---|
| Premises | £100,000 | Capital | £240,000 |
| Inventory | £2,600 | Reserves | |
| Debtors | £3,600 | Retained profit | £5,200 |
| Bank | £139,000 | | |
| | £245,200 | | £245,200 |

The business receives £2,400 that it is owed by some of its debtors and pays what is owed to its suppliers on day 11. The balance sheet will now be as in Example 11. The only change on the sources side is the disappearance of the creditor for £2,000 because payment has been made. On the uses side, the debtors are reduced by the £2,400 that they have paid and the bank balance is increased by £400 (£2,400 − £2,000); the premises and inventory remain unchanged.

You will have noticed that nothing that happens to a business can ever have only a single impact on the balance sheet. If this were not the case, the balance sheet would never balance and would serve no useful purpose. As has already been noted, the balance sheet, by its very nature, should always balance, and so each transaction that takes place must have more than one effect on it. Transactions may have seven impacts or more but never just a single one, and this is the basis of the double-entry system of bookkeeping that has been employed since the time of the Phoenicians. When we accountants see a good thing we know how to cherish it!

*Example 10b, redrawn business sheet*

Business balance sheet as at day 10

| Uses: | £ | £ | Sources: | £ |
|---|---|---|---|---|
| Fixed uses | | | | |
| Premises | | £100,000 | Capital | £240,000 |
| Fixtures/fittings | | | Reserves: | |
| Motor vehicles | | | Retained profit | £5,200 |
| | | | Loans | |
| Current uses: | | | Current sources: | |
| Inventory | £2,600 | | Creditor | £2,000 |
| Debtors | £6,000 | | | |
| Bank | £138,600 | £147,200 | | |
| | | £247,200 | | £247,200 |

Some conventions have been followed in constructing the balance sheets, and these should be explained in a little more detail. The 'sources' and 'uses' sides are each arranged in order of permanence, with the most permanent item at the top and the least permanent at the bottom. The uses are divided into fixed, which are retained in the business to earn profits (such as land and buildings), and current, which are consumed in order to earn profits (inventory and money, for example). The sources are allocated between permanent, consisting of capital and reserves, long-term, consisting of loans, and current, which includes creditors. The balance sheet takes the form shown in Example 10b when these conventions are employed.

These divisions between fixed and current uses and between permanent, long-term and current sources become important when we start to look at the interpretation of financial information by the personnel manager.

Another convention that is normally followed is for sources to be called 'liabilities'. This is because everything on that side is technically held by the business on somebody else's behalf. The capital and reserves belong to the owner(s) of the business, the loans consist of money that belongs to the lenders, and creditors are the people who supplied the credit, so that everything on that side is a liability of the undertaking.

The uses are called 'assets' because they are owned by the business. The premises, inventory and bank balance are all owned by the business, and the debtors are obliged to pay the business, so that their debt is owned by it. Using this new but more usually accepted terminology, the balance sheet takes the form shown in Example 10c.

The fixtures and fittings and motor vehicles have been included as examples of fixed assets; the loans would be an example of a long-term liability and accruals of a

*Example 10c, redrawn business sheet*

### Business balance sheet as at day 10

| Uses: | £ | £ | Sources: | £ |
|---|---|---|---|---|
| Fixed assets: | | | Capital | £240,000 |
| Premises | £100,000 | | Reserves: | |
| Fixtures/fittings | | | Retained profit | £5,200 |
| Motor vehicles | _____ | £100,000 | Loans | |
| Current uses: | | | Current liabilities: | |
| Inventory | £2,600 | | Creditor | £2,000 |
| Debtors | £6,000 | | Accruals | _____ |
| Bank | £138,600 | £147,200 | | |
| | | £247,200 | | £247,200 |

*Example 10d, balance sheet, vertical arrangement*

### Business balance sheet as at day 10

| | £ | £ |
|---|---|---|
| Fixed assets: | | |
| Premises | 100,000 | |
| Fixtures and fittings | | |
| Motor vehicles | _____ | 100,000 |
| | | |
| Current assets: | | |
| Inventory | 2,600 | |
| Debtors | 6,000 | |
| Bank | 138,600 | |
| | 147,200 | |
| | | |
| *Less* current liabilities | | |
| Creditors | 2,000 | |
| Accruals | _____ | |
| Net current assets (working capital) | | 145,200 |
| Net assets employed (net capital employed) | | 245,200 |
| Financed by: | | |
| Capital | 240,000 | |
| Reserves | 5,200 | 245,200 |
| Owner's equity | | 245,200 |

short-term liability, although nothing is yet shown against them. Accruals are sums due to be paid for items such as rent, rates and electricity.

The balance sheets that we have discussed so far have been in the two-sided form because they facilitate explanation, but most organisations publish their balance sheets in a vertical form, so we will redraw the above balance sheet in that form to illustrate the approach (Example 10d).

Organisations prefer to publish the balance sheet in the vertical (or, as it is sometimes called, the narrative) form because they believe it to be easier for the layperson to understand than the two-sided form. Items that are considered to be important, like the net current assets (working capital) and net assets employed (net capital employed) are highlighted and can be further explored should the need arise. This will be further discussed in Chapter 8 when we look at the interpretation of financial information.

When an organisation turns itself into a limited company, the major impact in the balance sheet is under the 'Capital' heading. If the business decided, through its formation documentation, that it would have the authority to issue 800,000 shares of £1.00 each and, in fact, issued 245,200 shares to the owner in return for the owner's equity, then the net assets employed (net capital employed) would be exactly as illustrated above, and total £245,200, but the 'Financed by' section becomes:

| *Financed by* | £ |
|---|---|
| Authorised capital: | |
|    800,000 shares of £1.00 each | <u>800,000</u> |
| Issued capital: | |
|    245,200 shares of £1.00 each | <u>245,200</u> |
|    Reserves | – |
|    Owner's equity | 245,200 |
|    Loans | <u>–</u> |
| | <u>245,200</u> |

The share capital of 245,200 shares of £1.00 has replaced the original owner's equity, which consisted of capital and reserves. This is to compensate the owner for the work that has to be carried out in starting up a business.

The following questions are for you to attempt before you check against the suggested answers provided at the back of the book.

## Exercise 1

Sacha has inherited £60,000 and intends to use it to fulfil a lifelong dream of setting up in business. On 5 June the money is paid into the business bank account. Draw up the balance sheet as at 5 June.

## Exercise 2

On 6 June Sacha obtains premises for £80,000, of which £40,000 is paid from the business bank account by cash, and the other £40,000 is borrowed. Draw up the balance sheet as at 6 June.

## Exercise 3

On 7 June fixtures and fittings of £8,000 are bought for cash. A small van that has been in Sacha's possession, worth £1,500, is brought into the business. Draw up the balance sheet as at 8 June.

## Exercise 4

The business is now ready to start trading, so on 8 June Sacha buys inventory for £30,000, of which £20,000 is a credit purchase and the balance is paid in cash. Draw up the balance sheet as at 8 June.

## Exercise 5

Sacha sells inventory that cost £20,000 for £60,000 on 9 June. £50,000 of the sales were on credit and the balance for cash. Draw up the balance sheet as at 9 June.

## Exercise 6

The business is doing so well that on 10 June Sacha decides to turn it into a limited company, and issues 203,000 shares at 50p for the owner's equity. Draw up the balance sheet to show how it would appear after this transaction, in both the two-sided and vertical forms.

In every case the balance sheets show the position of the business at a particular date, and have been drawn up after the transactions have occurred, and so are used as historical documents. There is no reason why they should not be used as planning tools, showing the position it is planned for the business to be in at some specific future date. This will be further discussed in Chapter 15.

This chapter has demonstrated the structure of the balance sheet and its use in providing information to the human resources department to aid decision-making.

# SELF-TEST QUESTIONS

1. What is capital?
2. What are reserves?
3. What is the purpose of working capital?
4. Why would the human resources manager be concerned about a high level of debtors?
5. What does net capital employed represent?
6. What is authorised capital?

## Work-based assignment

Study your organisation's balance sheet. Compare the total reserves with the bank and cash figures. Explain why they differ.

# The Trading and Profit and Loss Account and the Human Resources Manager

## OBJECTIVE

At the end of this chapter the reader will understand the profit and loss account and cash statement, and their use in providing information to the human resources manager. The standards that this chapter is intended to develop are those of 'interpreting information from key financial statements and managing financial resources to achieve goals and objectives through the budgetary planning and control process'.

We have seen from the previous chapter that it is possible to draw up a fresh balance sheet after every transaction that takes place in an organisation, but with the number of transactions that take place, it would become extremely cumbersome to do so. In order to overcome the problem we have to devise some means of collecting together transactions that would be helpful to those who need the information, as well as being meaningful in financial terms. This is achieved through the trading and profit and loss account.

The balance sheet shows the position of the business at a planned future date or at a specific date in the past. The trading and profit and loss account (sometimes referred to as the income statement) shows the results of an organisation's activities over a period of time, which may be a week, a month, several months, or a year, either as planned, or as occurred in the past. In preparing the trading and profit and loss account, several accounting principles have to be observed. These principles have to be followed to ensure that the accounts are prepared on a consistent basis from one year to the next. This makes them more useful to the human resources manager and others when they compare the results of several trading periods to ascertain the success or otherwise of the undertaking.

## ACCOUNTING PRINCIPLES

### The matching principle

This principle ensures that each accounting period stands alone and collects all the earnings and expenses related to it. There is a danger that when transactions overlap two accounting periods they will be counted twice, once in each period, or missed altogether. The matching principle helps to avoid this.

For example, assume that the profit and loss account is drawn up for the year from 1 January to 31 December, and that business rates of £1,000 are paid on 1 October for the six months to 31 March. Then the three months until 31 December will belong in one profit and loss account and the three months until 31 March will belong in the next. This is extremely important if the accounts are to be accurate enough to enable them to be used for purposes of comparison as well as recording the correct profit or loss.

A model of the organisation through time would be like Figure 6. If we did not have to manage the business, or pay taxes, or live, we would be able to wait until the end of its life before calculating the profit or loss that had been made. Unfortunately this is not possible, so each period's profit or loss has to be calculated. It is essential to ensure that all amounts which relate to that period are included and that any which relate to any other period are excluded. To achieve this happy result, many problems must be solved in the preparation of financial information.

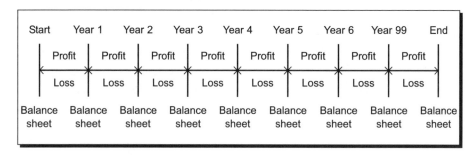

**Figure 6** *Organisational accounting through time*

## The principle of consistency

This helps in comparing performance in one financial period with that in another. If the methods employed when preparing the profit and loss accounts keep changing, comparison becomes impossible, so a decision must be made on how each item is to be dealt with. That method must continue to be used unless there is a very good reason for changing it.

An example is the way an organisation treats the charge for the use of fixed assets in the profit and loss account. Because of their nature, most fixed assets are expensive and last a long time. It would be unfair if one accounting period were charged for the whole of the cost of a fixed asset and the other periods had free use of it. The period in which the asset was bought would show a loss and the other periods a profit, as this example shows:

|  | £ | £ |
|---|---|---|
| Sales | 80,000 | |
| Cost of sales | <u>20,000</u> | |
| Gross profit | | 60,000 |
| Expenses | 40,000 | |
| New fixed asset | <u>100,000</u> | |
| | | <u>140,000</u> |
| Net loss | | <u>(£80,000)</u> |

In the next period, if the organisation just happened to achieve exactly the same performance, the accounts would show:

|  | £ |
|---|---|
| Sales | 80,000 |
| Cost of sales | <u>20,000</u> |
| Gross profit | 60,000 |
| Expenses | <u>40,000</u> |
| Net profit | <u>20,000</u> |

In order to avoid these wide fluctuations in profit we devise a means of charging a 'rent' for fixed assets, which we call depreciation. There are several ways of calculating the charge for depreciation. All are perfectly acceptable, but one that is most commonly used is the straight-line approach, which charges the same sum for the use of each specific asset over its life. To calculate the period charge for depreciation, three pieces of information are required: cost, life and scrap value.

If we have an asset that costs £101,000 which we estimate will last for 10 years and have a residual scrap value of £1,000, then the charge for depreciation is given by:

$$\frac{Cost - Scrap}{Life} = \frac{£101,000 - £1,000}{10 \ years}$$

$$= \frac{£100,000}{10 \ years} = £10,000 \ pa$$

|  | £ | £ |
|---|---|---|
| Sales | 80,000 | |
| Cost of sales | <u>20,000</u> | |
| Gross profit | | 60,000 |
| Expenses | 40,000 | |
| Depreciation on fixed asset | <u>10,000</u> | <u>50,000</u> |
| Net profit | | <u>£10,000</u> |

This irons out the fluctuations in profit and facilitates comparison of performance.

## The principle of conservatism

Accountants are by nature pessimistic. We feel it is better to look on the dark side and be surprised if things turn out better than expected, rather than to look on the bright side and be confounded if things turn out worse than expected. This is the principle of conservatism, under which we always anticipate losses but never profits. It is clearly demonstrated in the way in which inventory is valued.

Inventory is always valued at the lower of cost or current market value. If an item was purchased for £6,000 and its market value went up to £8,000, it would be valued in the accounts at £6,000. However, if its market value went down to £4,000, it would be valued in the accounts at £4,000.

## The principle of differentiating between capital and revenue items

Capital transactions involve fixed assets and affect the balance sheet, so that if we buy new machinery it appears under fixed assets in the balance sheet and the bank balance is reduced by the same amount. There is, at the time, no impact on the profit and loss account, but there will be at some later date, through the charge for depreciation.

Revenue transactions relate to running expenses like heating and lighting, rent and rates, wages and salaries, which have a direct impact on the profit and loss account but no direct effect on the balance sheet. They will, however, later affect the retained profit under the reserves.

## PROFIT

Having discussed the principles that are employed in the preparation of the trading and profit and loss account, let us see if we can decide what profit is and why it so often differs from cash. Profit may roughly be described as the earnings of the period concerned, whether or not they have been received, minus the expenses of the same period, whether or not they have been paid.

To take this a little further, profit may be illustrated as:

|  | £ | £ |
|---|---|---|
| Sales: | | |
| Credit | 80,000 | |
| Cash | 20,000 | |
| | | 100,000 |

Expenses:

| | | |
|---|---|---|
| Credit | 10,000 | |
| Cash | 50,000 | |
| | | 60,000 |
| Profit | | 40,000 |

The earnings are £100,000 and the expenses £60,000, giving a profit of £40,000, but what has been the effect on the bank balance? The bank balance has not, as we might have expected, been increased by the profit of £40,000 but reduced by £30,000. This is because the actual amounts of money have been:

| | £ |
|---|---|
| Payments for expenses | 50,000 |
| Receipts from sales | 20,000 |
| Net cash outflow | 30,000 |

The other transactions have involved credit, not cash. This shows that a profit of £40,000 has resulted in a cash reduction of £30,000, which highlights the important difference between profitability and liquidity, and helps to explain why so many profitable companies fail because they do not have the means to pay their way.

Let us look more closely at the trading and profit and loss account. We will use the illustration given in Example 2, on page 25. The statement could have been prepared historically on 15 October, or it could have been devised as a planning document and prepared on 1 May. Whatever its purposes, the principles on which it is prepared are exactly the same. To reinforce the point we will go through the entries item by item.

### Sales £600,000
This figure represents the total sales for the year and it is included whether or not any money has been received. Money received late on account of last year's sales would be excluded from this year's figure.

### Opening inventory £10,000
This is the stock that was left over, unsold, at the end of the previous trading period. It is valued at cost or current market value, whichever is the lower.

### Inventory purchased £360,000
This is the total purchases of stock for the year and is included whether or not the money has been paid. Money paid late on account of last year's purchases would be excluded from the figure.

### Closing inventory £50,000
This is the stock that has not been sold, valued at the lower of cost or current market value.

### Wages and salaries £150,000
This is the total that should have been paid during the year, taken from the wage records. Any wages that are due but unpaid would be included in this figure.

### Selling and distribution £20,000
This would include all the expenses that have been incurred during the year, whether they have been paid or not.

### Heating and lighting £10,000
This is the electricity, oil, gas, coal and so on that has been consumed during the year. Some apportionment may be necessary to ensure that only the expenses that relate to the year are borne by the year. This can be obtained from accounts received and metered readings.

### Depreciation £30,000
This will be the charge decided upon for the use of the fixed assets, as described under the principle of consistency. It is purely an apportionment of expenses and has no effect on money.

### Financing charges £30,000
This will be the total of the costs incurred in raising loans and the interest paid. It does not include the repayment of loans, which is a balance sheet item (a capital transaction).

### Miscellaneous £10,000
This will be the total of a whole series of sundry expenses, including telephone, postage, writing materials, refreshments and office cleaning.

### Net profit £30,000
This is the figure that, once it has been adjusted for things like taxation, will appear in the balance sheet under reserves.

## ADDED VALUE

So far we have discussed gross and net profit and you should have some understanding of the concepts involved. There is, however, an additional concept to which businesses and their owners attach great importance. This is 'added value', which illustrates how much an organisation is able to add to the costs incurred when arriving at the selling price of a product. The concept has been developed to such an extent that it is one of the factors used when assessing the strength of a company.

Added value is calculated in the following way:

| | |
|---|---|
| Sales turnover + other income | = Gross income |
| Gross income – Bought-out costs | = Added value |
| Added value – wage costs | = Net profit before tax |

Applying this to Example 2, page 25, we have:

| | £ | £ |
|---|---|---|
| Sales turnover | | 600,000 |
| *Less* materials | 320,000 | |
| Selling | 20,000 | |
| Heating | 10,000 | |
| Finance | 30,000 | |
| Miscellaneous | 10,000 | |
| | | 390,000 |
| Added value | | 210,000 |

The added value then goes to meet wage costs and depreciation. If there is any left when these costs have been met, it becomes profit.

The trading profit and loss account – and its relevance to the human resources manager as an aid to decision-making – will be explored more fully in Chapter 7 through the medium of the accounts of Marks & Spencer.

We have illustrated two kinds of financial statement: the balance sheet provides information about the position of a business at a given date; and the trading and profit and loss account (or income statement) shows the results of a period of activity in terms of profit. We will now concentrate on the cash statement, which shows what has happened to the money in the organisation and relates to the bank/cash in hand or overdrawn figure in the balance sheet. This is of great importance to the human resources manager as it shows whether or not there is sufficient money for the survival of the undertaking.

As is the case with the balance sheet and trading and profit and loss account, this statement can be prepared either for planning purposes or as a historical document, to show the results of past activities. When it is prepared for planning purposes on a daily, weekly or monthly basis, the cash statement becomes the cash budget, which is dealt with in detail in Chapter 16. In preparing the statement for past activities, we have to concentrate on the movements of money rather than the transactions that have taken place. For example, the sales of £600,000 in Example 2 on page 25 may consist of £400,000 cash and £200,000 credit; whilst £120,000 cash could have been received from credit sales in the previous year ending 31 July. Cash received would therefore be £520,000 and not the £600,000 shown as sales. We need to look at each entry in Example 2 and arrive at its cash equivalent in order for the cash statement to be prepared. This will further emphasize the difference between profitability and liquidity.

- *Opening inventory.* No cash movement.
- *Add inventory purchased.* This depends on what has been paid. It could be that £300,000 was for cash and £60,000 on credit, but a further £100,000 could have been paid for previously purchased items so that the payment would be £400,000 (£300,000 + £100,000) and not the £360,000 shown.
- *Less closing inventory.* No cash movement.
- *Wages and salaries.* These would all be paid, £150,000.
- *Selling and distribution.* There could be some outstanding payments, say £6,000, and £3,000 could have been paid for the previous year's outstanding, making the cash movement £17,000 (£20,000 + £3,000 – £6,000)
- *Heating and lighting.* Some of these accounts could be waiting to be paid, say £8,000, and £6,000 relating to last year could have been paid. This would make the cash £8,000 (£10,000 + £6,000 – £8,000).
- *Depreciation.* No cash movement. Depreciation is purely an apportionment of costs and does not increase cash movements.
- *Financing charges.* This depends on what has been paid. If all the charges have been paid, together with £6,000 from the previous year, the cash movement would be £36,000.
- *Miscellaneous.* There is possibly £2,000 due to be paid for last year's expenses, making the cash movement £12,000.

There could well be other items that are not shown in this profit and loss account which would affect the cash balance. For example, the purchase of a new fixed asset, like machinery, for £80,000 would have a big impact, and had the owner drawn any money from the business for his or her own purpose, that would have affected the cash but might well not have been included in salaries. If the owner is not paid a salary, then any money he or she draws is treated as if the owner were reclaiming some of the resources that were due from the business. On the other hand, if the owner is paid a salary for working in the business it is shown under salaries and not treated as drawings.

The historical cash statement drawn up on the above figures, assuming the opening balance was £4,000, becomes Example 12.

The result of the activities has been a profit of £30,000. But at the same time there has been a cash outflow of £103,000 (ie £623,000 – £520,000) which, after deducting the opening balance of £4,000, leaves an overdraft of £99,000 – once again emphasising that profitability does not equal liquidity.

Bear in mind that no matter how large or small an organisation is or whether it is in the public or the private sector, exactly the same principles are employed when the cash statement is prepared. The cash statement of a large manufacturing concern would include the items illustrated in Example 13.

*Example 12*

### Cash statement of 'X Co.' for the year ending 31 July

| | £ | £ |
|---|---|---|
| Opening balance in hand/(overdrawn) | | 4,000 |
| *Add* receipts from cash sales | | 400,000 |
| *Add* receipts from previous credit sales | | 120,000 |
| Total cash available | | 524,000 |
| | | |
| *Less* cash payments: | | |
| Goods purchased for cash | 300,000 | |
| *Add* payments for previous credit purchases | 100,000 | |
| Wages and salaries | 150,000 | |
| Selling and distribution | 17,000 | |
| Heating and lighting | 8,000 | |
| Finance charges | 36,000 | |
| Miscellaneous | 12,000 | 623,000 |
| Closing cash in hand (overdrawn) | | (99,000) |

*Example 13*

### Cash statement

| | £(000) | £(000) |
|---|---|---|
| Opening balance | 40 | |
| *Add* receipts | | |
| Money from trading | 40,000 | |
| Investments receipts | 100 | |
| | | 40,140 |
| *Less* payments: | | |
| Raw materials | 1,020 | |
| Fuel and light | 80 | |
| Factory wages | 22,144 | |
| Administrative salaries | 12,256 | |
| Carriage outwards | 250 | |
| Business rate | 2,300 | |
| General office expenses | 80 | |
| Repairs | 59 | |
| Financing costs | 121 | |
| | | 38,310 |
| Closing balance in hand | | 1,830 |

Individual departments within an organisation can also have their own cash statements, since it is necessary for each manager to control his or her departmental cash situation. This is discussed in detail in Chapter 16, but the statement of a typical human resources department would look something like Example 14.

*Example 14*

### Human resources department cash statement

| | £(000) | £(000) |
|---|---|---|
| Opening balance | 20 | |
| Share of organisational budget | 180 | |
| Externally provided training courses | 90 | |
| Inter-departmental training charges | _40_ | 330 |
| | | |
| Payments: | | |
| Salaries | 190 | |
| Recruitment costs | 60 | |
| Training costs | 60 | |
| Heat and light | 5 | |
| Telephone, postage | 8 | |
| Service charge | _7_ | _330_ |
| Balance | | ===== |

Do you feel a balanced cash statement is the sign of a good human resources manager?

This chapter has explained the profit and loss account and the cash statement and has demonstrated their use to human resource practitioners as an aid to decision-making.

The following exercises relate to chapters 4–7 and are for you to attempt before comparing your answers with the suggested solutions that follow.

## Exercise 7

Thomas has £5,000 with which to make a living and decides to become a market stall holder. He buys a pair of scales that cost £586, will last for an estimated six years and have a scrap value of £40, and a market stall on wheels that cost £1,140, will last an estimated four years and have a scrap value of £100. During his first four weeks' trading he buys second-grade fruit out of his original £5,000 for £2,600. At the end of the four weeks he has £3,800 left out of his takings after paying out:

|  | £ |
|---|---|
| Rent of yard | 120 (£40 per week) |
| Weekend help | 180 |
| Obstruction fines | 140 |

At the end of the period he owes £40 rent and has fruit left unsold which cost £240. He considers half the fruit to be still saleable. Calculate the profit for the period, the cash statement and the balance sheet at the end.

## Exercise 8

At the start of his second four weeks' operations Thomas is in the following position:

|  | £ |
|---|---|
| Inventory of saleable fruit costing | 120 |
| Cash in hand | 4,474 |
| One week's rent owing | 40 |
| A stall and a pair of scales | |

In the second four weeks he buys £3,900 of fruit for cash. He decides, after consulting his accountant, that he should spend £400 on household expenses. He takes out a loss-of-profits insurance policy at the beginning of the period, payable in advance, at an annual premium of £208. Other cash transactions during the four weeks are:

|  | £ |
|---|---|
| Rent | 120 (three weeks) |
| Fines | 260 |
| Help | 180 |
| Cash takings | 5,000 |

Closing value of inventory at cost is £500, half of which is in good condition and half of which he thinks will fetch only £150 (three-tenths of cost). What is his profit for the period, his cash balance and his financial position at the end of the second period? He finds he needs more to cover household costs. Can he afford it?

## Exercise 9

Thomas's position at the start of the third four weeks is:

|  | £ |
|---|---|
| Two weeks' rent owing | 80 |
| Insurance pre-paid | 192 |
| Inventory of fruit | 400 |
| Cash in hand | 4,406 |
| A pair of scales and the stall | 1,672 |

During the four weeks he buys fruit for £5,000 cash and feels that he can increase his household expenditure to £600. He does so and retains the balance of the money in the business. Other payments and receipts during the four weeks are:

|  | £ |
|---|---|
| Rent | 200 (five weeks) |
| Fines (one prosecution is pending. |  |
| The fine is expected to be £300) | nil |
| Weekend help | 180 |
| Cash takings for the month | 6,000 |

On the last day of the period he purchased a delivery van for £5,100 and sold his stall for £800. The value of his closing inventory was £600 at cost price. What was Thomas's profit for the period? Was there a profit or a loss on the sale of the stall? What is his financial position at the end of the period?

## Exercise 10

Thomas starts his fourth four weeks with:

|  | £ |
|---|---|
| Cash in hand | 126 |
| Provision for parking fine | 300 |
| Rent owing | 40 |
| Fruit unsold | 600 |
| Insurance pre-paid | 176 |
| Van | 5,100 |
| One pair of scales |  |

He senses that he is running into a cash-flow problem but his household costs are rising and so he increases the allocation to £650. The magistrates fine him £140 for the outstanding case of obstruction, and he decides to expand his business by starting a delivery round on the first day of the period, selling fresh vegetables with the fruit. He expects to keep the van for three years and then sell it for £810. His suppliers agree to let him open a credit account and the following transactions take place during the fourth four weeks:

|                                                                                                      | £     |
| ---------------------------------------------------------------------------------------------------- | ----- |
| Total cash purchases                                                                                 | 3,500 |
| Total purchases on credit                                                                            | 3,000 |
| Cash takings                                                                                         | 6,100 |
| Sales on credit to families whom he feels he can trust and who have promised to pay him next month   | 400   |
| Inventory of fruit and vegetables at the end of the period at market value                           | 1,700 |

His other cash transactions during the four weeks are:

|                         | £     |
| ----------------------- | ----- |
| Vehicle running expenses | 100   |
| Annual vehicle licence   | 130   |
| Rent paid                | 160   |
| Weekend help             | 180   |
| Payments to creditors    | 1,800 |

What is Thomas's profit for the period? What is his financial position at the end of the period? Does it accurately represent the worth of the business?

## SELF-TEST QUESTIONS

1. How do you calculate profit?
2. How do you calculate liquidity?
3. What is gross profit?
4. What is net profit?
5. What is most important to the human resources manager, cash or profit?

## Work-based assignment

Draw up a cash statement for your department and discuss its content with an accountant to reinforce your learning.

# The Manufacturing Account and the Human Resources Department

## OBJECTIVE

At the end of this chapter the reader will understand the preparation of the manufacturing account and its use to the human resources manager as a source of information. The management standard that this chapter will help to develop is 'interpreting information from key financial statements'.

Organisations that manufacture their own goods for sale require an additional financial statement to provide information on the cost of the goods that are being made. This helps to ensure that the manufacturing manager is able to maintain control over the operation and that the correct information is provided to facilitate good decision-making. The manufacturing account comes before the trading and profit and loss account, and collects together all the costs of manufacture. These are transferred to the trading and profit and loss account in the 'cost of goods sold' section, where it replaces 'inventory purchased'. We shall explore this more fully as we work through Example 16, but it is important to remember that the manufacturing account is part of the management information system and can either be prepared historically or used as a planning tool. The manufacturing sector of the UK economy is much smaller than it was prior to the 1970s, when major changes took place in its structure. This has meant that greater emphasis has been placed on the service sector but manufacturing is essential to the survival of UK Ltd and has to be nurtured if we are to maintain our important position in the world economy.

The manufacturing account contains a great deal of information about wages and salaries, both direct and indirect, that are of interest to human resources. Direct wages relate to those people who are directly involved in the manufacturing process ie those who actually make something. Indirect wages relate to those who are not actually producing anything like supervisors, cleaners and maintenance people.

Example 15 shows a manufacturing account, which contains useful information for management. It can be made even more useful if it is broken down into the cost per unit produced, as we will see in Chapter 10. The way in which the manufacturing account fits in with the trading and profit and loss accounts will be developed later, but in order to clarify the situation, let us first look at each item in the manufacturing account in turn.

*Example 15*

| Manufacturing account of 'Makes Co.' for the year ending 30 June | | |
|---|---|---|
| | £ | £ |
| Opening inventory of raw materials | 40,000 | |
| *Add* raw materials purchased | 810,000 | |
| | 850,000 | |
| *Deduct* closing inventory of raw materials | 60,000 | |
| Raw materials consumed | | 790,000 |
| Direct manufacturing wages | | 1,410,000 |
| Direct expenses | | 10,000 |
| Prime/direct cost of goods made | | 2,210,000 |
| *Add* indirect factory expenses/overheads | | |
| Salaries and wages | 70,000 | |
| Materials | 30,000 | |
| Heating and lighting | 40,000 | |
| Rent and rates | 60,000 | |
| Depreciation | 90,000 | |
| | | 290,000 |
| Total manufacturing costs | | 2,500,000 |
| *Add* opening work in progress | | 10,000 |
| | | 2,510,000 |
| *Deduct* closing work in progress | | 20,000 |
| Cost of finished goods made | | 2,490,000 |

- *Opening stock of raw materials.* The raw materials that are available to be used at the beginning of the financial period. They are valued at the lower of cost or current market value.
- *Raw materials purchased.* The raw materials purchased during the financial period under review. They need not necessarily have been paid for.
- *Closing stock of raw materials.* The raw materials that are left unused at the end of the financial period. They become the opening stock of raw materials for the new period and are valued at the lower of cost or current market value.
- *Raw materials consumed.* The raw materials that have actually been used in the manufacturing process.
- *Direct manufacturing wages.* The wages of the people who are directly involved in making the product. It includes the machine operators but excludes supervisors and packers.
- *Direct expenses.* Expenses that can be identified with a particular product, and which increase as the number of units produced increases. An example would be power metered separately to a machine making a single product. There are often no direct expenses in a manufacturing concern.

- *Indirect factory expenses/overheads*. Expenses that are not identified with a particular product and generally remain fixed irrespective of the number of items that are produced. It is often difficult to arrive at the total to be charged to the manufacturing account, as opposed to the trading and profit and loss account. For example, a small manufacturing concern may have one rates bill for the whole site, and then have to apportion it between the manufacturing and non-manufacturing areas.
- *Salaries and wages*. The remuneration paid to the factory manager, supervisors, cleaners and others whose time is spent in the manufacturing area.
- *Materials*. The cost of materials used in the area that do not go directly into the product. They include such things as cleaning materials, packaging and general-issue items like screws.
- *Heating and lighting*. The cost of heating and lighting the factory or workshop area. If there is one bill for the whole premises, some apportionment between the manufacturing and non-manufacturing areas will be necessary.
- *Rent and rates*. This is the cost of rent and rates relating to the factory or workshop. Some apportionment will be necessary between the manufacturing and non-manufacturing areas if they are not billed separately.
- *Depreciation*. The charge for the use of machinery, equipment, buildings and other fixed assets in the manufacturing area.
- *Total manufacturing costs*. The total cost, collected together in the manufacturing account, of all the items that have been produced.

The relationship of the manufacturing account to the trading and profit and loss accounts can be illustrated as shown in Example 16.

There would also be deductions for tax but the amount would depend on the current tax legislation, which changes every year, and is therefore beyond the scope of this book.

The manufacturing account is used to ensure that the costs of manufacturing are properly controlled and that wastage is kept to a minimum. Correctly and promptly prepared accounts ensure that management is fully conversant with the current situation and able to take corrective action quickly when it proves to be necessary. If, for example, the production manager had evidence that raw material costs were escalating because of theft, she or he would liaise with the personnel manager to ensure that the correct procedures were being followed.

It may be that the organisation finds that the demand for its manufactured product is price-sensitive, and that a competitor is selling an equivalent item more cheaply. This will cause market share to be lost and management will have to decide on how to combat the threat. The manufacturing account should provide sufficient detail for the cost of each item manufactured to be calculated. Comparison with the competitor's

*Example 16*

Trading and loss and profit account of 'Makes Co.' for the year ending 30 June

| | £ | £ |
|---|---|---|
| Sales | | 7,600,000 |
| Less cost of goods sold: | | |
| Opening inventory of finished goods | 40,000 | |
| *Add* costs of goods manufactured (From the manufacturing account) | 2,490,000 | |
| | 2,530,000 | |
| *Deduct* closing inventory of finished goods | 30,000 | |
| Cost of finished goods sold | | 2,500,000 |
| Gross profit | | 5,100,000 |

This is the end of the trading account. We then go on to the profit and loss account section:

| | £ | £ |
|---|---|---|
| Gross profit | | 5,100,000 |
| *Less* expenses: | | |
| Wages and salaries | 3,750,000 | |
| Selling and distribution | 250,000 | |
| Heating and lighting | 40,000 | |
| Depreciation | 120,000 | |
| Financing charges | 65,000 | |
| Miscellaneous | 15,000 | |
| | | 4,240,000 |
| Net profit before tax | | 860,000 |

selling price of the product will indicate to the management the courses of action that are open to it. Where the competitor's price is higher than the manufacturing cost it might be possible to reduce the selling price in order to reclaim lost market share. If, on the other hand, the manufacturing cost is higher than the competitor's selling price then management has a major problem to resolve.

The selling price could be reduced below the cost price in the hope of recovering market share and possibly forcing the competitor out of business, but this is an extremely high-risk strategy and could not be pursued for a long period unless the organisation is financially strong. A second option would be to investigate ways of reducing manufacturing costs so that the selling price could be brought down.

The human resources manager might well be closely involved in this process, since a common way of controlling costs is by reducing staff numbers and counselling is often provided to those made redundant. In the event that neither of these strategies proves possible, a search would be made for a new product or products into which it might be worth diversifying. The last resort would be to endeavour to sell the organisation as a going concern before it was forced into liquidation.

Example 15 shows that the cost of goods made was £2,490,000. If that cost was for manufacturing 800,000 units then the cost per unit would be:

$$£2,490,000 \div 800,000 = £3.11$$

A competitor coming to the market with a similar product selling at £10 would not, under normal circumstances, present a major threat. On the other hand one coming into the market at £5 would be a major problem, particularly as the product is at present selling for £9.46 (assuming sales of 803,215 units to achieve the sales value of £7,600,000 shown in the accounts).

This chapter has explained the manufacturing account and its use to human resources practitioners as a tool to facilitate good decision-making.

## SELF-TEST QUESTIONS

1. How is the manufacturing account of use to human resources?
2. What are direct expenses?
3. What is prime cost?
4. Why is the manufacturing account an aid to pricing?
5. How does the manufacturing account link with the trading account?
6. How might the human resources manager become involved if production costs are shown to be too high?

## Work-based assignment

Obtain the manufacturing account of two organisations and compare the information provided. Do they appear to have been prepared on the same basis? Which do you consider to be the easier to understand?

# The Interpretation and Use of Financial Information for Human Resources

## CHAPTER 7

## OBJECTIVE

At the end of this chapter you will understand the purpose of ratios and their application in assessing the performance of organisations from the point of view of the human resources manager. The management standards that will be developed are 'managing financial resources to achieve goals and objectives through the budgetary planning and control process, interpreting information from key financial statements and analysing financial and other information used in making outsourcing decisions'.

In the preceding chapters we have investigated the financial information that is provided by the management information system, and noted the danger of information being received too late to be useful. Assuming that the organisation has ensured that the correct information is reaching the right person quickly enough to be used, we will look at some of the ratios that will help personnel make better use of it in planning and control.

The ratios breakdown into three main areas: profitability, liquidity and efficiency or activity. We will investigate each in turn, using the account of 'Trader Co', Example 17.

## PROFITABILITY RATIOS

These control ratios are concerned with the return on the long-term investment in the organisation – that is, the return on the capital employed – and with the return on the sales, showing how much the sales contribute to fixed costs (those that do not change with the level of activity, like salaries) and whether there is enough left over for a profit.

We will look first at the return on the capital employed. The most accepted measure of capital employed is the 'net capital employed', which is the total assets minus the current liabilities.

### Gross profit as a percentage of the net capital employed

This is calculated using the formula:

$$\frac{\text{Gross profit} \times 100}{\text{Net capital employed}} = \frac{£490,000 \times 100}{(£7,250,000 - £50,000)} = \frac{£49,000,000}{£7,200,000} = 6.8\%$$

## Managing Financial Information

*Example 17*

### Trading and profit and loss account of 'Trader Co.' for the year ending 31 August

| | £ | £ |
|---|---|---|
| Sales | | 960,000 |
| Less cost of goods sold: | | |
| Opening inventory of finished goods | 12,000 | |
| *Add* finished goods manufactured | 488,000 | |
| | 500,000 | |
| *Deduct* closing inventory of finished goods | 30,000 | |
| Cost of finished inventory sold | | 470,000 |
| Gross profit | | 490,000 |
| *Less* expenses: | | |
| Wages and salaries | 150,000 | |
| Selling and distribution | 75,000 | |
| Heating and lighting | 45,000 | |
| Depreciation | 70,000 | |
| Financing charges | 35,000 | |
| Miscellaneous | 15,000 | |
| | | 390,000 |
| Net profit | | 100,000 |

### Balance sheet of Trader Co. as at 31 August

| | £ | £ | | £ | £ |
|---|---|---|---|---|---|
| Fixed assets: | | | | | |
| Land and buildings | | 4,050,000 | Capital | | 4,600,000 |
| Plant and machinery | 3,864,000 | | Reserves: | | |
| *Less* depreciation | 1,800,000 | | Retained profit | | 875,000 |
| | | 2,064,000 | Loan | | 1,725,000 |
| Fixtures and fittings | 1,266,000 | | | | |
| *Less* depreciation | 200,000 | | | | |
| | | 1,066,000 | | | |
| Motor vehicles | 65,000 | | | | |
| *Less* depreciation | 45,000 | 20,000 | | | |
| | | 7,200,000 | | | |
| Current assets: | | | Current liabilities: | | |
| Inventory | 30,000 | | Creditors | 40,000 | |
| Debtors | 20,000 | | Accruals | 10,000 | |
| Bank | 0 | | | | |
| | | 50,000 | | | 50,000 |
| | | 7,250,000 | | | 7,250,000 |

This figure in isolation is of little or no value, but if a trend over five years is obtained we can see whether management is able to exercise control over the organisation's operations. In this example the gross profit is largely dependent on the difference between the buying price and the selling price, and once a figure has been accepted as reasonable for the gross profit as a percentage of the net capital employed it should not alter significantly unless the management decides that it should. If a return of 6.7 per cent is considered acceptable and over five years the actual results have been 6.6 per cent, 6.7 per cent, 6.7 per cent, 6.8 per cent and 6.8 per cent, then analysts would be happy that, at least with regard to the buying and selling of goods, the organisation was operating satisfactorily. On the other hand, a set of results showing 6.0 per cent, 7.2 per cent, 5.8 per cent, 6.3 per cent and 7.0 per cent would leave a serious question mark over the management of the undertaking.

Whenever performance is being measured it should be remembered that one figure in isolation is useless. Only a set of results showing a trend over five years or so can be meaningful, and the average for the industry or business sector, which can be found in publications like 'Dunn and Bradstreet', would be helpful.

## Net profit as a percentage of the net capital employed

This is often referred to as the primary ratio, and is calculated using the formula:

$$\frac{\text{Net profit} \times 100}{\text{Net capital employed}} = \frac{£100,000 \times 100}{(£7,250,000 - £50,000)} = \frac{£10,000,000}{£7,200,000} = 1.4\%$$

This figure shows the overall return on the long-term investment in the business and can be compared with the return that could be earned from investing the money safely in a bank, building society or national savings & investments. Clearly 1.4 per cent is far less than could be earned almost anywhere else with the money. Using this criterion, the result for the year is poor. To discover whether it is a freak result we need the average for the last five years as well as the average for the business sector in which the concern operates. If it is a true representation of the return the organisation makes, then in purely financial terms it should be closed down and the money invested where it would earn a higher return. There may, however, be good reasons for remaining in the business, which might be providing a valuable service, or the owners may enjoy what they are doing so much that they do not wish to close. It is always dangerous to make decisions on limited information, but ratios do highlight areas that require investigation.

## Gross profit as a percentage of sales

This is calculated using the formula:

$$\frac{\text{Gross profit} \times 100}{\text{Sales}} = \frac{£490,000 \times 100}{£960,000} = 51\%$$

This figure is a useful control ratio, as it represents the difference between the buying price and the selling price of the goods; once it has been decided upon, it should not alter from period to period. Again, it is of little use in isolation, but a trend over five or more years will reveal much about the way in which the undertaking is being controlled. The gross profit as a percentage of sales is a reflection of the 'mark-up', the amount that has been added to the cost price of the goods to arrive at the selling price. The calculation of the mark-up is (selling price – cost price) as a percentage of the cost price, which in this example is:

$$\frac{(£960,000 - £470,000) \times 100}{£470,000} = \frac{£490,000 \times 100}{£470,000} = 104.3\%$$

This is to say that the concern is adding 104.3 per cent to the cost price of the goods to arrive at the selling price. This may sound a lot, but it should be remembered that all the running costs of the organisation as well as the profit have to be met out of this figure. The selling price minus the cost price divided by the selling price gives the sales margin which is an important control ratio in retail. In this example it is:

$$\frac{(£960,000 - £470,000) \times 100}{£960,000} = \frac{£490,000 \times 100}{£960,000} = 51\%$$

which is the same as the gross profit as a percentage of sales, but this will not always be the case as gross profit is not necessarily the difference between the cost price and the selling price of the goods. Differences might occur for example when there is wastage.

## Net profit as a percentage of sales

This is calculated using the formula:

$$\frac{\text{Net profit} \times 100}{\text{Sales}} = \frac{£100,000 \times 100}{£960,000} = 10.4\%$$

This represents the percentage of sales that is left over for profit once all the other expenses have been met. When compared with the average for the industry and a trend over five or more years it is possible to see whether the undertaking is performing better or worse than average, and whether it is improving or deteriorating with time. In common with all ratios, this one does not provide a definitive answer but indicates where it may be necessary to investigate further. Even activities like recruitment and training are inextricably linked with profitability ratios (hence the need for the human resources manager to understand them and always keep in mind the position of the business). After all, when an organisation is failing to make good use of its resources there is little point in recruiting additional people who may shortly have to be released;

and staff who require training often need help defining their needs, which always depends on the likely future direction of the whole business.

# LIQUIDITY RATIOS

These are concerned with an undertaking's ability to pay its way in the medium and short-term future. Like all other ratios, they do not indicate much about the organisation when taken on their own, but used in conjunction with the average for the sector and the trend over the last five or more years they become good indicators of overall liquidity.

## Current ratio

This is given by current assets as a ratio of current liabilities, with the current liabilities represented as unity (1). In our example, we have current assets of £50,000 and current liabilities of £50,000. To express this as a ratio, we have current assets:current liabilities, and this becomes £50,000:£50,000. Since the current liabilities are always shown as 1, to arrive at the figure for the current assets we divide the current assets by the current liabilities:

$$\frac{\text{Current assets}}{\text{Current liabilities}} = \frac{£50,000}{£50,000} = 1$$

So we have the current ratio of 1:1.

This indicates the firm's ability to pay its way in the medium term: that is, about four to nine months into the future. We can see that the current assets just cover the current liabilities but have no indication as to whether that is good or bad. Some organisations, like Kidde in the manufacturing sector, have a current ratio of 2.7:1, whereas Tesco Stores has a current ratio of 1.3:1, so it is important to know the average for the sector and the trend for this ratio, where changes may be far more important than the actual figure.

## Quick ratio (acid test)

This is given by the quick assets as a ratio of the current liabilities. The 'quick' assets are those that can be readily turned into cash. These obviously exclude fixed assets and normally also exclude the figure for inventory. In the example, we have quick assets of £20,000 and current liabilities of £50,000, giving a quick ratio or acid test of:

$$20,000:50,000 = \frac{£20,000}{£50,000} :1 = 0.4:1$$

This indicates a firm's ability to pay its way in the short term (ie up to four months in the future). The ratio seems extremely low, but when compared with such companies as Sainsbury's and Tesco, which run on low quick ratios of approximately 0.2:1, it appears less of a problem.

Looking at the balance sheet, we see that there is no money and that there are relatively low debtors of £20,000 against creditors of £40,000. Much depends on how quickly inventory can be turned into money, and it would be interesting to see the trend over the last five or more years, but certainly alarm signals are flashing and further investigation is required into the short-term liquidity of the Trader Co.

## The long-term solvency ratios, gearing and interest cover

The long-term solvency ratio, often referred to in the United Kingdom as the gearing ratio and in the US as the leverage, is of great importance to human resources managers and others. The higher the gearing, that is to say the greater the borrowing as a proportion of the total long-term financing, the higher the risk of business failure. This is due to the fact that money is a valuable asset that has to be paid for through interest: the more the borrowing, the greater the amount of money that has to be found. This can lead to cash-flow problems when profits fall, and even possible business failure. There is currently great concern about the purchase of Manchester United because of the huge amount of debt that will be involved, incurring interest charges of £126,164 per day at current estimates. Management should borrow enough to benefit the business but not so much as to cause problems; it is here that the gearing ratio can be helpful. If an organisation's gearing ratio is below the average for the business sector, no major problems should ensue. On the other hand, if it goes above the average, alarms should sound and questions should be asked.

Interest cover is another long-term solvency ratio, and is becoming more popular than the gearing ratio. It is calculated by dividing the profit before interest by the interest charged. Trends are important but if the ratio falls below 1.5, an investigation should be undertaken to ascertain the cause of the problem.

## EFFICIENCY RATIOS OR ACTIVITY RATIOS

Efficiency ratios indicate how effectively the inventory, creditors and debtors of the concern are being managed. The latter all form part of the working capital, which, remember, is current assets minus current liabilities. Lack of working capital means that the organisation cannot be run effectively, so it has to be carefully managed. There are three efficiency ratios that will be considered.

## Rate of inventory turnover, or age of inventory

This tells the organisation how many times the inventory is changed in a year, or how long on average it is held before being used. The objective of most undertakings is to hold as little inventory as possible for as short a time as possible. The advent of the 'just in time' system of inventory management is an attempt to hold no inventory at all but to buy stock as it is needed. This is proving extremely difficult to achieve in practice but there is certainly a strong move towards it. Money tied up in inventory is regarded by many as dead money that could be put to better use elsewhere.

In calculating the speed with which inventory is being used we employ the formula: cost of inventory used, divided by the year-end inventory or, where there is sufficient information, the average inventory holding during the period under review. A rough average inventory holding is given by:

$$\frac{\text{Opening inventory + Closing inventory}}{2}$$

Trader Co. has opening inventory of £12,000 and closing inventory of £30,000, which gives an average inventory of:

$$\frac{£12,000 + £30,000}{2} = \frac{£42,000}{2} = £21,000$$

The cost of inventory used is cost of finished inventory sold, £470,000, so the number of times the inventory has been turned over is given by dividing £470,000 by £21,000, ie 22 times a year. It is therefore held on average for:

$$\frac{52}{22} : 2.4 \text{ weeks}$$

This would be regarded as quite fast for most concerns, but a petrol retailer or fast food shop would be very unhappy with it, so again we need to look at the average for the sector and the trend over the last five or more years before we can begin to draw any conclusions.

## Speed of turnover of creditors, or age of creditors

This indicates how many times the creditors are turned over (not physically!) in the year, or how many weeks they are kept waiting for their money. Most managers try to ensure that they are not paying their suppliers any more quickly than they receive money from their customers.

In calculating the speed with which we pay our suppliers, we apply the formula: credit purchases (if the credit purchases are not known the total purchases figure is used) divided by the year-end creditors. Using the figures in our example, we have £488,000 divided by £40,000: 12 per year. This shows that on average they have had to wait

52/12 = 4.3 weeks for their money. This is very quick by today's standards. Most concerns keep their suppliers waiting more than 4.3 weeks, but once again the figure should be treated with care and should be compared with the trend over five or more years, the industry average and the speed with which money is collected from customers.

## Speed of turnover of debtors, or age of debtors

This indicates the number of times the debtors are turned over in the year, or how many weeks they take to pay for the goods they have received from the undertaking. The formula used is credit sales (if known; otherwise the total sales figure is used) divided by the year-end debtors. Using the figures in our example, we have £960,000 divided by £20,000. This means we have collected money from our customers approximately 48 times in 52 weeks, showing that on average the organisation has had to wait approximately one week for its money. (Using the alternative convention of working in days and assuming 360 working days in a year, 360/48 = 7.5 days, which again indicates that virtually all the sales are converted into cash in one week).

We can now investigate the quick ratio or acid test further in the light of this new information. The acid test was 0.4:1, which appeared to indicate short-term liquidity problems, but we now know that sales are converted into cash within a week, and suppliers are kept waiting four weeks for their money. Assuming sales take place evenly throughout the year, the daily value of goods sold is:

$$\frac{£960,000}{360} = £2,667$$

In other words, the creditors of £40,000 could be paid from 15 days of sales, so what at first sight appears to be a serious liquidity problem turns out to be more manageable when additional information is available.

The liquidity and efficiency ratios are key indicators that enable management to ensure that the organisation will survive and is successfully meeting the operating targets. Since the human resources manager is often an important member of the executive team, present at meetings where critical decisions are made, a good knowledge of the financial ratios is essential if he or she is to contribute fully to the discussion.

## Z-score predicting corporate failure

We have seen that there are a number of financial ratios that can be used by human resources managers to help them understand the health of the undertaking, but sometimes it is a little difficult to decide which ratio should be acted upon. To help overcome this problem Altman (1968), Marais (1982) and Robertson (1983) amongst others, developed the Z-score approach, which attempts to identify key ratios for analysing organisational performance and rank them according to their perceived importance. Marais, who worked on data from Britain, looked at 40 ratios before settling on four that he considered to be critical. It is important to remember that the ratios selected are the choice of one man, and other analysts use different ones. This applies whichever method of calculating the Z-score is chosen.

There is some consistency between the methods in that the formula used is in general terms similar to that employed by Altman. That is:

$$Z = 1.2(A) + 1.4(B) + 3.3(C) + 1(D) + 0.6(E)$$

Where   A = working capital/assets
            B = retained earnings/assets
            C = pre-tax earnings/assets
            D = sales/assets
            E = market value of equity/liabilities

Altman considers an undertaking that has a Z-score of less than 1.81 to be at risk of going into liquidation. This ratio appears to be more sophisticated than the others that we have studied but is subject to exactly the same limitations, and it would be dangerous to use it in isolation. The human resources manager should look at trends and what is happening to other liquidity ratios before attempting to draw any conclusions about the health of the concern. The Z-score provides useful information for the human resources manager to help in decision-making and providing advice. It can be provided by the accountant should it be required so we will not demonstrate its calculation in this book.

This chapter has explained the major ratios and indicated their strengths as aids to human resource practitioners in understanding organisational performance and in facilitating decision-making. It has also emphasised the danger of relying too much on a single indicator in an economic climate that is continuously changing. JJB Sports and Kingfisher have recently warned of a downturn in demand in the high street; the CBI has cut its growth forecasts and Sir Ken Morrison has been forced by City and shareholder pressure to hand over the day-to-day running of Morrison Supermarkets to a new chief executive because of a failure to meet profit targets. On the other hand ITV bucked the trend with an upbeat advertising forecast. Marks & Spencer reported a 19 per cent slump in profits and the chief executive, Marcus Rose, has been told he must do better but Burberry, a market leader, reported an 18 per cent increase in profits. In the end, whatever information is available, the success or failure of the enterprise depends on good decision-making by management.

## Exercise 11

Apply these ratios where possible to Exercises 7–10 at the end of Chapter 5 and state whether you feel things are improving or deteriorating. Then compare your answers with the suggested ones given at the end of the book.

We have considered the ratios of fictitious organisations and seen how they are calculated. It is important for human resources managers to understand them and their purpose so that they can use them to reinforce any points that they may wish to make either in discussions with individuals or in meetings. Let us now apply what we have learned to the accounts of Sainsbury's (extracts following).

## SAINSBURY PLC
### Group profit and loss account
for the 52 weeks to 29 March 2003

| | 2003 £m | 2002 £m |
|---|---|---|
| **Turnover including VAT and sales tax**[A] | 18,495 | 18,206 |
| VAT and sales tax | (1,065) | (1,044) |
| Continuing operations | 17,430 | 17,154 |
| Discontinued operations | – | 8 |
| **Turnover excluding VAT and sales tax** | 17,430 | 17,162 |
| Cost of sales (including exceptional costs | (16,039) | (15,905) |
| **Gross profit** | 1,391 | 1,257 |
| Group administrative expenses (including exceptional costs) | (717) | (632) |
| **Continuing operations – operating profit before exceptional costs and amortisation of goodwill** | 752 | 679 |
| Exceptional operating costs | (65) | (38) |
| Amortisation of goodwill | (13) | (14) |
| **Continuing operations – operating profit** | 674 | 627 |
| **Discontinued operations – operating loss** | – | (2) |
| **Group operating profit** | 674 | 625 |
| Share of profit/(loss) in joint ventures | 3 | (1) |
| Loss on sale of properties | (11) | (4) |
| Disposal of operations – discontinued | 61 | – |
| **Profit on ordinary activities before interest** | 727 | 620 |
| Net interest payable and similar items | (60) | (49) |
| **Underlying profit on ordinary activities before tax**[B] | 695 | 627 |
| Exceptional items | (15) | (42) |
| Amortisation of goodwill | (13) | (14) |
| **Profit on ordinary activities before tax** | 667 | 571 |
| Tax on profit on ordinary activities | (206) | (200) |
| **Profit on ordinary activities after tax** | 461 | 371 |
| Equity minority interest | (7) | (7) |
| **Profit for the financial year** | 454 | 364 |
| Equity dividends | (298) | (285) |
| **Retained profit for the financial year** | 156 | 79 |
| **Basic earnings per share** | 23.7p | 19.1p |
| **Underlying earnings per share**[B] | 24.2p | 21.5p |
| **Diluted earnings per share** | 23.7p | 18.9p |
| **Underlying diluted earnings per share**[B] | 24.1p | 21.3p |

A Including VAT at Sainsbury's Supermarkets and sales tax at Shaw's Supermarkets.

B Before exceptional items and amortisation of goodwill.

## SAINSBURY PLC
### Balance sheets
at 29 March 2003 and 30 March 2002

| | Group 2003 £m | Group 2002 £m | Company 2003 £m | Company 2002 £m |
|---|---|---|---|---|
| **Fixed assets** | | | | |
| Intangible assets | 226 | 263 | – | – |
| Tangible assets | 7,540 | 6,906 | 368 | 471 |
| Investments | 112 | 174 | 7,667 | 6,285 |
| | 7,878 | 7,343 | 8,035 | 6,756 |
| **Current assets** | | | | |
| Stock | 800 | 751 | – | – |
| Debtors | 297 | 398 | 111 | 208 |
| Sainsbury's Bank's current assets | 2,397 | 2,193 | – | – |
| Investments | 20 | 16 | – | – |
| Cash at bank and in hand | 639 | 370 | 242 | 1 |
| | 4,153 | 3,728 | 353 | 209 |
| **Creditors: amounts falling due within one year** | | | | |
| Sainsbury's Bank's current liabilities | (2,237) | (2,060) | – | – |
| Other | (2,537) | (2,648) | (467) | (747) |
| | (4,774) | (4,708) | (467) | (747) |
| **Net current liabilities** | (621) | (980) | (114) | (538) |
| **Total assets less current liabilities** | 7,257 | 6,363 | 7,921 | 6,218 |
| **Creditors: amounts falling due after more than one year** | (1,885) | (1,223) | (3,567) | (1,907) |
| **Provisions for liabilities and charges** | (300) | (231) | (52) | (29) |
| **Total net assets** | 5,072 | 4,909 | 4,302 | 4,282 |
| **Capital and reserves** | | | | |
| Called up share capital | 484 | 484 | 484 | 484 |
| Share premium account | 1,424 | 1,421 | 1,424 | 1,421 |
| Revaluation reserve | 22 | 39 | – | – |
| Profit and loss account | 3,073 | 2,904 | 2,394 | 2,377 |
| **Equity shareholders' funds** | 5,003 | 4,848 | 4,302 | 4,282 |
| Equity minority interest | 69 | 61 | – | – |
| **Total capital employed** | 5,072 | 4,909 | 4,302 | 4,282 |

The financial statements were approved by the Board of Directors on 20 May 2003, and are signed on its behalf by

**Sir Peter Davis** *Group Chief Executive*
**Roger Matthews** *Group Finance Director*

## SAINSBURY PLC
### Group flow statement
for the 52 weeks to 29 March 2003

|  | 2003 £m | 2002 £m |
|---|---|---|
| **Net cash inflow from operating activities** | 1,070 | 1,067 |
| Dividend received from joint venture | 8 | – |
| **Returns on investments and servicing of finance** | | |
| Interest received | 67 | 66 |
| Interest paid | (108) | (114) |
| Interest element of finance lease payments | (21) | (21) |
| Net cash outflow from returns on investments and servicing of finance | (62) | (69) |
| **Taxation** | (224) | (171) |
| **Capital expenditure and financial investment** | | |
| Purchase of tangible fixed assets | (1,169) | (1,070) |
| Sale of tangible fixed assets | 130 | 218 |
| Purchase of intangible fixed assets | (3) | (3) |
| Net cash outflow from capital expenditure and financial investment | (1,042) | (855) |
| **Acquisitions and disposals** | | |
| Repayments of loans to joint ventures | 27 | – |
| Investment in joint ventures and fixed asset investments | (1) | (6) |
| Proceeds from sale of subsidiary undertakings | – | 3 |
| Proceeds from disposal of other fixed asset investments | 184 | – |
| Net cash inflow/Coutflow) for acquisitions and from disposals | 210 | (3) |
| **Equity dividends paid to shareholders** | (288) | (275) |
| **Net cash outflow before use of liquid resources and financing** | (328) | (306) |
| **Financing** | | |
| Issue of ordinary share capital | 3 | 17 |
| Decrease in short-term borrowings | (88) | (116) |
| Increase in long-term borrowings | 550 | 434 |
| Increase in finance leases | 151 | – |
| Capital element of finance lease payments | (5) | (4) |
| Net cash inflow from financing | 611 | 331 |
| **Increase in net cash** | 283 | 25 |
| **Reconciliation of net cash flow to movement in net debt** | | |
| Increase in net cash | 283 | 25 |
| Increase in debt and lease financing | (462) | (314) |
| Movement in finance leases | (156) | (8) |
| Exchange adjustments | 87 | – |
| Movement in net debt in the year | (248) | (297) |
| **Net debt at the beginning of the year** | (1,156) | (859) |
| **Net debt at the end of the year** | (1,404) | (1,156) |

### 3. Analysis of operating profit

| | 2003 | 2002 | | |
| --- | --- | --- | --- | --- |
| | Continuing operations | Continuing operations | Discontinued operations | Total |
| | £m | £m | £m | £m |
| Turnover | 17,430 | 17,154 | 8 | 17,162 |
| Cost of sales | (15,988) | (15,867) | (10) | (15,877) |
| Exceptional cost of sales | (51) | (28) | – | (28) |
| Gross profit | 1,391 | 1,259 | (2) | 1,257 |
| Administrative expenses | (690) | (608) | – | (608) |
| Exceptional administrative expenses | (14) | (10) | – | (10) |
| Amortisation of goodwill | (13) | (14) | – | (14) |
| Group administrative expenses | (717) | (632) | – | (632) |
| Operating profit | 674 | 627 | (2) | 625 |

The exceptional operating costs comprise the following:

| | 2003 | 2002 |
| --- | --- | --- |
| | £m | £m |
| Sainsbury's Supermarkets | 51 | 20 |
| Shaw's Supermarkets | – | 8 |
| Exceptional cost of sales | 51 | 28 |
| Sainsbury's Supermarkets | 4 | 10 |
| Shaw's Supermarkets | 10 | – |
| Exceptional administrative expenses | 14 | 10 |
| Total exceptional operating costs | 65 | 38 |

The costs in Sainsbury's Supermarkets relate to the Business Transformation Programme which involves upgrading its IT systems, supply chain and store portfolio. These costs are exceptional operating costs due to the scale, scope and pace of the transformation programme. These costs primarily relate to asset write offs and reorganisation costs. The cost of closure of the Taste joint venture of £5 million in 2002 is also included in Sainsbury's Supermarkets' exceptional administrative expenses for that year.

At Shaw's Supermarkets, the exceptional costs relate to costs associated with the acquisition of stores from the liquidator of Ames during the year. Exceptional cost of sales for Shaw's Supermarkets in 2002 relates to the closure of a depot.

### 4. Loss on sale of properties

| | 2003 | 2002 |
| --- | --- | --- |
| | £m | £m |
| Loss on disposal of Sainsbury's Supermarkets' properties | (7) | (5) |
| (Loss)/profit on disposal of Shaw's Supermarkets' properties | (4) | 1 |
| | (11) | (4) |

## 5. Disposal of operations – discontinued

|  | 2003 £m | 2002 £m |
|---|---|---|
| Disposal of investment In Homebase | 61 | – |

The Group sold its remaining investment in Homebase Limited and redeemed the outstanding loan notes in the year for a total consideration of £184 million. The profit on sale of the investment, after making provision for further liabilities arising from sites associated with the sale in 2001, amounted to £61 million.

## 6. Net interest payable and similar items

|  | 2003 £m | 2002 £m |
|---|---|---|
| Interest receivable | 45 | 79 |
| Interest payable and similar charges: |  |  |
| Bank loans and overdrafts | 2 | 3 |
| Other loans | 97 | 120 |
| Finance leases | 28 | 21 |
|  | 127 | 144 |
| Interest capitalised |  |  |
| – tangible fixed assets | (20) | (12) |
| – land held for and in the course of development | (2) | (4) |
|  | 105 | 128 |
| Net interest payable and similar items | 60 | 49 |

Total interest receivable amounted to £171 million (2002: £202 million), including interest receivable attributable to Sainsbury's Bank of £126 million (2002: £123 million) included in sales. Total interest payable amounted to £199 million (2002: £224 million) including interest payable attributable to Sainsbury's Bank of £72 million (2002: £80 million) included in cost of sales. Interest is capitalised at the weighted average cost of related borrowings.

## 7. Profit on ordinary activities before tax

|  | 2003 £m | 2002 £m |
|---|---|---|
| Profit on ordinary activities before tax is stated after charging/(crediting): |  |  |
| Depreciation of tangible fixed assets |  |  |
| – owned assets | 348 | 350 |
| – assets under finance leases | 45 | 8 |
| Amortisation of intangible assets | 18 | 18 |
| Employee costs | 1,913 | 1,910 |
| Pension costs | 73 | 71 |
| Operating lease rentals |  |  |
| – properties | 275 | 252 |
| – fixtures, equipment and vehicles | 6 | – |
| – receivable | (29) | 26 |

The Auditors' remuneration for audit services amounted to £0.6 million (2002: £0.5 million) for the Group including £0.1 million (2002: £0.1 million) for the Company. The Auditors also received £1.4 million (2002: £2.2 million) for non-audit services relating to consultancy fees for strategic (£0.6 million), regulatory (£0. 1 million) and taxation (£0.7 million) advice.

73

## 8. Employees

|  | 2003<br>£m | 2002<br>£m |
|---|---|---|
| Employees' and Executive Directors' remuneration and related costs during the year amounted to: |  |  |
| Wages and salaries | 1,739 | 1,735 |
| Social security costs | 101 | 104 |
| Other pension costs | 73 | 71 |
|  | 1,913 | 1,910 |

|  | 2003<br>Number<br>000's | 2002<br>Number<br>000's |
|---|---|---|
| The average numbers of employees during the year were: |  |  |
| Full-time | 54.2 | 53.4 |
| Part-time | 120.3 | 121.3 |
|  | 174.5 | 174.7 |
| Full-time equivalent | 108.7 | 108.5 |

## Sainsbury's accounts

| 1. **Profitability Ratios** | | 2002 | 2003 |
|---|---|---|---|

A. Gross profit to net capital employed

| | | | |
|---|---|---|---|
| $\dfrac{\text{Gross Profit} \times 100}{\text{Net capital employed}}$ | $\dfrac{1257 \times 100}{6363} =$ | 19.8% | 19.2% |

B. Net Profit to Net Capital Employed

| | | | |
|---|---|---|---|
| $\dfrac{\text{Profit on Ordinary Activities Before Tax} \times 100}{\text{Net capital employed}}$ | $\dfrac{571 \times 100}{6363} =$ | 9.0% | 9.2% |

C. Gross Profit Percentage of Sales

| | | | |
|---|---|---|---|
| $\dfrac{\text{Gross Profit} \times 100}{\text{Sales}}$ | $\dfrac{1257 \times 100}{18206} =$ | 6.9% | 7.5% |

D. Net Profit Percentage of Sales

| | | | |
|---|---|---|---|
| $\dfrac{\text{Net Profit} \times 100}{\text{Sales}}$ | $\dfrac{571 \times 100}{18206} =$ | 3.1% | 3.6% |

## 2. Short Term Liquidity Ratios
A. Current Ratio

| | | | |
|---|---|---|---|
| Current Assets:Current Liabilities | 3728:4708 = | 0.79:1 | 0.87:1 |

B. Quick Ratio

| | | | |
|---|---|---|---|
| Quick Assets:Current Liabilities | 2961:4708 = | 0.63:1 | 0.70:1 |

## 3. Long Term Solvency Ratio

A. Gearing Ratio

| | | | |
|---|---|---|---|
| $\dfrac{\text{Borrowing} \times 100}{\text{Equity}} =$ | $\dfrac{1223 \times 100}{4848} =$ | 25.2% | 37.7% |

B. Interest Cover

| | | | |
|---|---|---|---|
| $\dfrac{\text{Profit before interest}}{\text{Interest}} =$ | $\dfrac{620}{49} =$ | 12.6 times | 12.1 times |

| 4. **Efficiency or Activity Ratios** | | **2002** | **2003** |
|---|---|---|---|

A. Collection period for debts (Age of Debtors)

| | | 2002 | 2003 |
|---|---|---|---|
| Turnover | $\frac{18206}{82}$ = 222 times | 1.6 days | 2.3 days |
| Trade debtors | | | |

B. Payment period for Creditors (Age of Creditors)

| | | 2002 | 2003 |
|---|---|---|---|
| Cost of Sales | $\frac{15905}{2023}$ = 7.9 times | 46.2 days | 49.3 days |
| Trade Creditors  = | | | |

C. Rate of Stock Turnover

| | | 2002 | 2003 |
|---|---|---|---|
| Cost of Sales | $\frac{15905}{586}$ = 27.1 times | 13.5 days | 15.0 days |
| Year End Stock | | | |

D. Fixed Asset Turnover

| | | 2002 | 2003 |
|---|---|---|---|
| Turnover (Sales) | $\frac{18206}{6906}$ | 2.6 times | 2.4 times |
| Tangible Fixed Assets | | | |

E. Number of Employees (Note 8)   108700

Sales per Employee

Turnover (Sales)
Number of Employees

| | | 2003 |
|---|---|---|
| | $\frac{18495 \text{ million}}{108700}$ = | £170,147 |

Once you have calculated the ratios what have they told you about Sainsbury's? What information would be helpful in getting a feel for the company's performance?

# Exercise 12

Using the accounts of 'World Games plc' shown below, calculate the profitability, liquidity and efficiency ratios, and employ them to assess its financial performance. How would you as the human resources manager employ this information?

## World Games PLC

Mr. Davies is Managing Director of World Games plc, manufacturers of electronic games equipment. He is reviewing the progress of his company, which he established 10 years ago in Cardiff. It is a public company and he plans to obtain a Stock Exchange quotation in about two years' time. In view of this Mr. Davies believes he should increase his dividend as much as possible; no interim dividends are paid, only the final dividend.

He is an inventive man and a first-class electronic engineer. He has an excellent and fast-growing development and design department, and in the last three years he has produced some extremely sophisticated equipment. The number of new items is now eight times what it was three years ago. He prides himself that his company could design almost anything that a customer would require in electronic games equipment. This viewpoint is well founded, for the company has a good reputation for inventive skills and is often consulted by agencies.

His sales force has more than doubled over the last three years, and he now has a back up team of seven, covering the United Kingdom and abroad. His customers are widely spread both geographically and in terms of customers served.

His manufacturing has become efficient and he has doubled his output whilst his staff numbers have only increased marginally. The stock figures in the balance sheet represent materials and components; there is no finished work.

Despite this apparent success his bank manager, who has just received the company's latest profit and loss account and balance sheet, has asked him to call at the bank at 1600 hrs on Wednesday 30 March, as the bank is seriously concerned with the state of his company. The overdraft has risen to £180,000 at close of business on Monday 28 March and the bank wants it to be considerably reduced. In September of last year the overdraft limit was increased from £100,000 to £160,000.

The accounts and operating data of World Games for the last three years of operation are shown below.

Critically assess the company's performance and state what action you feel Mr. Davies should take.

**World Games plc**
Balance sheet, 31 December 2002

| | £ | £ | £ |
|---|---|---|---|
| Fixed assets: | | | |
| Buildings | | 182,054 | |
| Plant | | 120,265 | |
| Vehicles | | 8,162 | 310,481 |
| Current assets: | | | |
| Work in progress | 106,203 | | |
| Stocks of raw materials | 71,019 | | |
| Debtors | 105,001 | | |
| Bank | 1,050 | 283,273 | |
| Current liabilities | | | |
| Creditors | 32,546 | | |
| Tax | 30,664 | 63,210 | |
| Working Capital | | | 220,063 |
| NET CAPITAL EMPLOYED | | | 530,544 |
| FINANCED BY | | | |
| Issued capital and reserves | | | |
| 340,000 50p ordinary shares | | | 170,000 |
| General reserves | | | 300,000 |
| Share premium account | | | 30,327 |
| Balance profit and loss account | | | 30,217 |
| | | | 530,544 |

**World Games plc**
Balance sheet, 31 December 2003

| | £ | £ | £ |
|---|---|---|---|
| Fixed assets: | | | |
| Buildings | | 215,056 | |
| Plant | | 463,472 | |
| Vehicles | | 9,890 | 688,418 |
| Current assets: | | | |
| Work in progress | 176,321 | | |
| Stocks of raw materials | 110,984 | | |
| Debtors | 154,986 | | |
| Bank | 1,283 | 443,556 | |
| Current liabilities: | | | |
| Creditors | 43,625 | | |
| Tax | 35,331 | | |
| Dividends 10 per cent | 27,000 | 105,956 | |
| Working Capital | | | 337,600 |
| NET CAPITAL EMPLOYED | | | 1,026,018 |
| FINANCED BY: | | | |
| Issued capital and reserves | | | |
| 540,000 50p ordinary shares | | | 260,000 |
| Share premium account | | | 405,000 |
| General reserves | | | 300,000 |
| Balance profit and loss account | | | 51,018 |
| | | | 1,026,018 |

**World Games plc**

Balance sheet, 31 December 2004

| | £ | £ | £ |
|---|---|---|---|
| Fixed assets: | | | |
| Buildings | | 235,125 | |
| Plant | | 456,684 | |
| Vehicles | | 11,034 | 702,843 |
| Current assets: | | | |
| Work in progress | 246,105 | | |
| Stocks of raw materials | 171,864 | | |
| Debtors | 216,031 | 634,000 | |
| Current liabilities: | | | |
| Creditors | 53,201 | | |
| Tax | 44,852 | | |
| Dividends 15 per cent | 40,500 | | |
| Bank overdraft | 162,647 | 301,201 | |
| Working Capital | | | 332,800 |
| NET CAPITAL EMPLOYED | | | 1,035,643 |
| FINANCED BY: | | | |
| Issued capital and reserves | | | |
| 540,000 50p ordinary shares | | | 270,000 |
| Share premium account | | | 405,000 |
| General reserves | | | 300,000 |
| Profit and loss account | | | 60,643 |
| | | | 1,035,643 |

**World Games plc**

Profit and loss account, year ended 31 December

| | 2002 | | | 2003 | | | 2004 | | |
|---|---|---|---|---|---|---|---|---|---|
| | £ | £ | £ | £ | £ | £ | £ | £ | £ |
| SALES | | 500,607 | | | 699,231 | | | 899,698 | |
| DIRECT COSTS | | | | | | | | | |
| Materials | 115,321 | | | 153,875 | | | 186,436 | | |
| Labour | 70,653 | | | 87,487 | | | 103,502 | | |
| | | 185,974 | | | 241,362 | | | 289,938 | |
| INDIRECT | | | | | | | | | |
| COSTS | | | | | | | | | |
| Salaries | 27,000 | | | 31,800 | | | 35,000 | | |
| Wages | 38,200 | | | 68,500 | | | 100,200 | | |
| Materials | 13,500 | | | 29,500 | | | 45,500 | | |
| Tools | 6,500 | | | 8,500 | | | 10,500 | | |
| Expenses | 12,280 | | | 17,568 | | | 22,940 | | |
| Depreciation | 14,300 | | | 34,000 | | | 57,000 | | |
| Heating | 19,000 | | | 23,000 | | | 24,000 | | |
| | | 130,780 | | | 212,868 | | | 295,140 | |
| TECHNICAL | | | | | | | | | |
| DEPARTMENT | | | | | | | | | |
| Salaries | 20,820 | | | 33,700 | | | 51,490 | | |
| Wages | 4,840 | | | 8,860 | | | 10,400 | | |
| Materials | 1,800 | | | 4,770 | | | 5,200 | | |
| Expenses | 7,684 | | | 11,201 | | | 13,267 | | |
| Depreciation | 960 | | | 1,590 | | | 2,100 | | |
| | | 36,104 | | | 60,121 | | | 82,457 | |
| SALES | | | | | | | | | |
| DEPARTMENT | | | | | | | | | |
| Technical Reps | 7,185 | | | 11,108 | | | 17,863 | | |
| Expenses | 2,835 | | | 4,682 | | | 6,947 | | |
| Exhibitions | 6,243 | | | 9,235 | | | 15,386 | | |
| Advertising | 3,820 | | | 6,461 | | | 7,010 | | |

| | 2002 | | | 2003 | | | 2004 | | |
|---|---|---|---|---|---|---|---|---|---|
| | £ | £ | £ | £ | £ | £ | £ | £ | £ |
| Salaries | 4,187 | | | 6,914 | | | 8,964 | | |
| Expenses | 6,600 | | | 10,350 | | | 13,100 | | |
| Depreciation | 212 | | | 240 | | | 415 | | |
| | | 31,082 | | | 48,990 | | | 69,685 | |
| GENERAL | | | | | | | | | |
| ADMINISTRATION | | | | | | | | | |
| Managing director | 17,500 | | | 20,100 | | | 21,800 | | |
| Accounts dept | 11,890 | | | 15,040 | | | 17,740 | | |
| Other admin exp | 10,072 | | | 17,031 | | | 16,637 | | |
| Depreciation | 545 | | | 587 | | | 912 | | |
| Bank interest | − | | | − | | | 10,412 | | |
| | | 40,007 | | | 52,758 | | | 67,501 | |
| TOTAL COSTS | | | 423,947 | | | 616,099 | | | 804,721 |
| PROFIT | | | 76,660 | | | 83,132 | | | 94,977 |

# SELF-TEST QUESTIONS

How would the human resources manager employ the following ratios?

1. Gross profit to net capital employed.
2. Net profit percentage sales.
3. Interest cover.
4. Rate of stock turnover.
5. Sales per employee.
6. Debtors' ratio.
7. Creditors' ratio.

## Work-based assignment

Obtain the accounts of your concern and assess its performance over two recent years. Decide whether you feel it is improving, and highlight its strengths and weaknesses.

# Financial Implications of Human Resource Decisions

## CHAPTER 8

## OBJECTIVE

At the end of this chapter you will understand the financial implications of human resource decisions and some of the ways in which they can be calculated. The management standards that will be developed are 'managing financial resources to achieve goals and objectives through the budgetary planning and control process' and 'analysing financial and other information used in outsourcing decisions.'

The main decisions of the human resources manager concern personnel but there are others which are important, as for example the purchase of capital equipment or the offering of training services outside the employing organisation. Each of these decisions will generate both costs and revenues and it is essential that the human resources manager fully appreciates their implications. A more detailed discussion of this important topic appears in Hugo Fair's *Personnel and profit*.

People are essential to the success of all organisations. They are the major asset of any undertaking, but they are also a major cost. It is because of this that it is important to ensure that organisations are using their people effectively, efficiently and economically. In the private sector a key ratio that is successfully employed is sales per employee (see the analysis of Sainsbury's accounts in Chapter 7). Do you know what this figure is in your business? You should be aware that if you recruit additional people it will have an immediate impact on the sales per employee ratio. This ratio, like the others we have discussed, should never be considered in isolation. Trends are significant, as are comparisons with other similar businesses. Using the manufacturing account example in Chapter 6 and assuming that there are 5,000 employees, we can calculate the sales per employee to be:

$$\frac{\text{Sales}}{\text{Employees}} \quad \frac{7,600,000}{5,000} = £1,520$$

If you were presented with this figure in isolation your reaction would probably be, 'so what!' In order to be meaningful it has to be compared with something. If sales per employee had been £2,000 for the last four years and suddenly fell to £1,520, you would want to know why and correct the situation if possible. Recruitment of additional staff would have an impact on the ratio unless you were immediately able to generate proportionally higher sales. For example, an extra 100 staff would make the sales per employee:

$$\frac{7,600,000}{5,100} = \text{£}1,490.20$$

This fall of nearly £30 per employee would have to be recovered as quickly as possible. Sales per employee of £1,520 are not sufficient to make a profit unless the average salary in the organisation is considerably below this figure. If it were not, there would be insufficient funds to pay staff especially when we remember that sales do not represent profit. In view of this it is unlikely that there would be 5,000 staff, but more likely 50, which would give sales per employee of £7,600,000 ÷ 50 = £152,000. If staff levels rose to 55, sales per employee would fall to :

$$\text{£}7,600,000 \div 55 = \text{£}138,181.81$$

which emphasises the importance of staff levels to organisations.

Sales are not as critical in the public sector as they are in the private sector, so the above ratio would not apply. But it might be replaced by such ratios as refuse collected, houses painted or meals served per employee.

This concentration on the activity per employee has led many organisations, and managers within them to believe that the way to save money and operate more effectively is by reducing the number of staff. There is a great emphasis on headcount and the human resources manager has to demonstrate the added value provided by staff, particularly in his or her own department. It is incumbent on the manager to provide information that demonstrates the efficiency of the department, and if this can be achieved through the use of ratios so much the better. One ratio that is commonly used for this purpose is the cost of human resources, which is calculated by dividing the total expenses of the organisation into the expenses of each department. If the expenses of an organisation are £6,740,000 and those of the human resources, manufacturing, sales and marketing departments are £960,000, £3,400,000, £1,230,000 and £1,150,000 respectively, then the ratio for each department becomes:

Human Resources $\quad \frac{\text{£}960,000}{\text{£}6,740,000} \times 100 = 14.2\%$

Manufacturing $\quad \frac{\text{£}3,400,000}{\text{£}6,740,000} \times 100 = 50.6\%$

Sales $\quad \frac{\text{£}1,230,000}{\text{£}6,740,000} \times 100 = 18.2\%$

Marketing $\quad \frac{\text{£}1,150,000}{\text{£}6,740,000} \times 100 = 17.1\%$

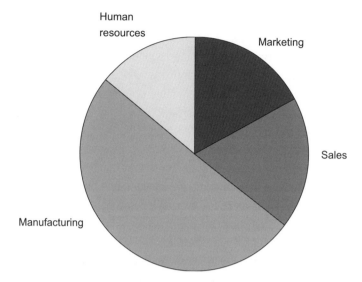

**Figure 7** *Pie chart*

This could then be illustrated in a pie-chart such as the one above.

To be able to undertake such an investigation, the human resources manager would require more information than is provided by the traditional financial accounts, and it is for reasons like this that the cost accounts, to which we will be introduced in the next chapter, were developed.

The capital investment decision has a major impact on the organisation: by its nature it uses a large proportion of the available money and may carry over for more than one financial year. If for example the human resources manager requires a new training wing costing £4 million, it is extremely unlikely that the proposal will be accepted unless the budgeted benefits can be seen to exceed the costs by a satisfactory amount. It is no use talking in general terms about the benefits that will accrue to the organisation from such a step. Estimates have to be made of the savings and/or income that will be generated by the scheme, and they must be compared with the outlay. The manager will then be able to build a case for the proposal and hopefully demonstrate its advantages over competing bids for the available funds for capital outlay. He or she can employ such tools as pay-back, which demonstrates how quickly the expenditure is recovered, and net present value, which compares the outlay with the estimate of funds to be generated in present value terms. These approaches are discussed in greater detail in Chapter 17.

Many organisations are now offering expertise that they previously employed internally to the open market. Training is one such service and it is reasonable that this should be done. Undertakings that have been proactive in training and development over the last six years have found that other organisations are prepared to pay well for their expertise. But the human resources manager should not embark on such a course of action without fully considering the attendant costs and benefits. There is more than one way of calculating the costs of such a venture. If the full-cost approach is adopted, all costs would have to be recovered plus the required profit. This approach is fully discussed in Chapter 11. On the other hand, the concept of contribution may be applied, using the marginal costing approach. Here only those costs directly involved in providing the additional training are considered; any income over and above that makes a contribution to the departmental fixed costs. Chapter 13 covers this approach in greater detail.

All human resource decisions have financial implications and managers need detailed financial information. The provision of this information is discussed in the remainder of the book.

This chapter has examined the ways in which financial information can contribute to human resource decision-making, but it must be remembered that the decision is always made by the human resources manager and not the information provided.

## SELF-TEST QUESTIONS

1. Why are people important to organisations?
2. What do you understand by added value?
3. What is the cost of human resources ratio?
4. Why are undertakings offering training on the open market?

## Work-based assignment

Ascertain the financial information that the human resources manager in your organisation considers to be the most important to enable him or her to make better decisions.

# Management Accounting and Human Resources Practitioners

# PART 2

# Introduction to
# Management Accounting

The financial accounts were sufficient to meet the needs of management until the middle of the last century when the rate of change in the world and particularly the public and private sectors accelerated at an ever-increasing rate. This meant that management needed more information to help in planning, decision-making and control. It used to be sufficient to prepare the financial accounts annually, but pressure on management meant that it was necessary to provide relevant information much more frequently: quarterly, monthly, weekly and in many instances, as with cash balances, daily. The human resources manager needs to know the amount of cash that is available to be spent by the department on a regular and frequent basis if overspending or underspending are to be avoided.

This section of the book will deal with costing as well as planning and control, and with their application to the human resources manager. Costing breaks down into: *absorption*, which deals with the way in which costs can be allocated to different parts of an undertaking; *standard*, which looks at how expected costs can be estimated, compares the actual cost with the estimate and helps decide what remedial action, if any, is necessary; and *marginal*, which helps the human resources manager justify plans for expenditure on new initiatives like providing training for other organisations.

Planning covers the overall planning system, which examines the total planning process and those involved, the impact of the environment on plans, and the ways in which changes can be managed to minimise their impact on the organisation. An important element of planning is the cash budget since any undertaking that runs out of money will fail, and it is here that we see the importance of control. It is of no earthly use for the human resources manager to suddenly discover that the department has run out of cash. A good system of control would have warned of the danger many weeks in advance so that action could be taken to avoid the situation. The master budget draws the separate parts of the plan into a cohesive whole, whilst the capital budget enables the manager to justify bids for money to support new developments like a state-of-the-art training centre.

These topics are comprehensively covered in a user-friendly way, with examples that help clarify important issues and demonstrate their utility to the human resources practitioner. It is important to remember that both sections of this book are essential to the human resources specialist who wishes to progress within the department or the wider organisation. It is extremely embarrassing to attend a meeting where financial information is presented of which you have no understanding. The fear is that you will be asked to express an opinion and will only be able to reiterate what others have said – unless you are the first one asked. The information contained in this book will ensure that does not happen, provided you take the time to read, enjoy and practise it.

# Costing and Human Resources

## CHAPTER 10

## OBJECTIVE

At the end of this chapter you will understand how cost accounts are prepared, their link with the financial accounts, and the human resources implications. The management standards that will be developed are 'managing financial resources to achieve goals and objectives through the budgetary planning and control process', 'interpreting information from key financial statements' and 'evaluating business plans for functional organisational projects'.

The information systems that have been dealt with so far have been concerned with financial information for planning and reporting, with some control elements. In Chapter 6 manufacturing accounts were discussed, and it was suggested that these lend themselves to calculating the cost per unit produced. Because information of this nature is the basis for exercising control in an organisation, it will be investigated more fully.

The accounts we have dealt with so far are the financial accounts that give an overview of the position of an organisation. Whilst this information can help human resources and other managers to control the finances for which they are responsible and to make bids for resources, more detailed information is required if costs are to be controlled and plans monitored. This is provided by the cost accounts, which must be capable of being reconciled with the financial accounts at all times. Costing is the process of analysing the expenditure of an organisation into the separate costs for each of the services or products supplied to customers, which will include training.

The way in which the cost and financial accounts may be reconciled can be shown simply in the Example 18.

Without the benefit of the cost accounts, the planning team might have been inclined to concentrate on cleaning, which generates the largest earnings. An examination of the cost accounts, however, clearly shows that training gives the greatest profit and might be an appropriate area to develop. Cost accounts then can assist the human resources manager in making a case for the contribution made by the department to the health of the organisation as a whole. But, as I have said, it is essential for the cost accounts to be reconciled with the financial accounts. If they are not they are no value to managers and their preparation is a waste of time.

*Example 18*

Financial and cost accounts

*Financial accounts*

|  |  | £(000) |
|---|---|---|
| Earnings | | 1,432 |
| Expenses | | 1,141 |
| Profit | | 291 |

*Cost accounts*

| | £(000) | £(000) | £(000) | £(000) | £(000) |
|---|---|---|---|---|---|
| *Service* | *Cleaning* | *Security* | *Training* | *Transport* | TOTAL |
| Earnings | 680 | 415 | 123 | 214 | 1,432 |
| Expenses | 630 | 372 | 9 | 130 | 1,114 |
| Profit | 50 | 43 | 114 | 84 | 291 |

The purposes of costing can be stated to be to:

■ enable work in progress and finished goods to be valued for short-term and annual accounts
■ provide the basis for tenders, pricing policies and estimates
■ maintain control over the costs of an organisation
■ provide information to ensure that decisions are made on the correct basis.

The costs of each department consist of three elements:

■ labour
■ materials
■ overheads.

These three elements of cost are further broken down into direct costs, which are charged directly to the service or product and indirect costs, which are apportioned to the service or product on some equitable basis, as discussed in Chapter 11. The cost accounts and the financial accounts are combined in the following way:

   Direct labour
+  Direct materials
+  Direct expense
_____
=  PRIME COST
+  Factory overhead
_____
=  PRODUCTION COST

+   Selling and distribution overhead
+   Selling and distribution direct expense
+   Administration overhead

= COST OF SALES taken from EARNINGS
= NET PROFIT

The manager also needs to know whether the costs with which she or he is dealing are fixed (that is, they remain constant for any level activity within prescribed limits) or variable (they vary directly with changes in the level of activity). An example of a fixed cost might be staff salaries in a department that employed three trainers, each capable of training between 10 and 20 people. Their combined salaries would be £60,000 whether they were training 30 people or 60 people a week. However, if they were asked to train 100 people a week, the departmental salary bill would become £100,000 because an additional two trainers would have to be employed. The fixed cost line on a graph would then appear as in Figure 8.

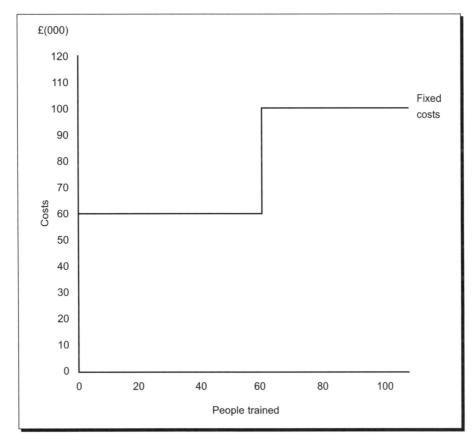

**Figure 8** *Fixed costs in a training department*

A variable cost would be the cost of the information pack and other materials given to each trainee on the programme. Taking the cost per trainee as £50, the variable cost line could be illustrated as in Figure 9.

You can see from this that if there were no trainees the cost would be zero, whilst for 100 the cost is £5,000. This is helpful to the human resources manager in costing the service provided against the revenues generated by it.

The next three chapters describe various costing methods and their application to the human resources manager. They also contain examples of the ways in which they can be calculated and used. It is essential for the human resources manager to fully understand and control the costs that relate to the human resources department.

This chapter has explored the preparation of the cost accounts, their relationship with the financial accounts, which is essential to their utility, and their human resources implications.

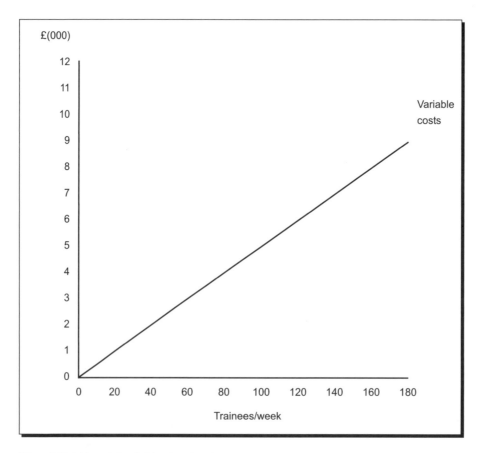

**Figure 9** *Variable costs in a training department*

## SELF-TEST QUESTIONS

1. What is a direct cost?
2. What is a fixed cost?
3. Why do cost accounts and financial accounts have to be reconciled?
4. What is the prime cost a total of?
5. Why are direct costs important?

## Work-based assignment

Ascertain the fixed and variable costs that relate to your department.

# Absorption costing

## CHAPTER 11

## OBJECTIVE

At the end of this chapter you will understand how fixed costs are apportioned to the human resources department, why the apportionment often gives rise to concern and the difference between absorption costing and activity-based costing. The management standards that will be developed are 'managing financial resources to achieve goals and objectives through the budgetary planning and control process' and 'analysing financial and other information used in making outsourcing decisions.'

Standard costing is useful in enabling managers to calculate the expected cost of a unit of production or service. Absorption costing, or total costing, as it is sometimes called, helps to ensure that organisational costs are fully recovered when a price is quoted for a job or a unit of consultancy. Because little can be done to alter fixed costs in the short term, they are often overlooked when prices are being calculated, with disastrous results for the organisation. We have seen that one example of a fixed cost is salaries. Others are financing charges, rents, business rates, heating and depreciation.

Variable costs include the materials used in making a product or providing a service. They also include any labour cost that is charged at an hourly rate for that job or service. These variable costs are relatively easy to control because they can be readily identified and action can be taken to correct the situation if they are seen to be moving in an unexpected way.

Semi-variable costs behave as though they are a combination of fixed and variable costs, with an element that is fixed and an element that alters with the level of activity. An example of such a cost would be maintenance, which has a planned fixed element whatever the level of activity and a variable element that alters with activity. Such costs are extremely difficult to identify.

### Example 19

We can now study an example illustrating the use of absorption costing through the medium of a manufacturing organisation which has two departments and a single product. During manufacture the product spends some time in each of the departments. The expected costs for a month are:

|  | £ |
|---|---|
| Business rates | 300 |
| Heating and lighting | 60 |
| Depreciation | 100 |
| Salaries | 6,000 |
| Administration | 400 |

The resources allocated to the two departments are:

| Department | A | B |
|---|---|---|
| Floor area (square metres) | 20 | 40 |
| Number of employees | 5 | 15 |
| Value of machinery (£000) | 40 | 10 |
| Production labour hours | 600 | 1,800 |

In order to calculate the amount that must be charged out by the departments for work done, the appropriate overhead cost has to be established. This is calculated by first of all apportioning the overhead costs to the departments on an equitable basis:

| Cost | Department | | Total | Basis of apportionment |
|---|---|---|---|---|
| | A | B | | |
| | £ | £ | £ | |
| Rates | 100 | 200 | 300 | Floor area |
| Heating and lighting | 15 | 45 | 60 | Number of employees |
| Depreciation | 80 | 20 | 100 | Value of machinery |
| Salaries | 1,500 | 4,500 | 6,000 | Labour hours |
| Administration | 100 | 300 | 400 | Number of employees |
| Total | 1,795 | 5,065 | 6,860 | |

The total overhead allocated to the departments is: department A, £1,795, department B, £5,065. It is now necessary to decide how the overheads are to be recovered. One way of doing this would be to calculate the amount of overhead to be charged for each labour hour of work done. To do this it is necessary to divide the overheads allocated to the department by the number of production labour hours expected in the department. Using the same example, we have:

| Department | A | B |
|---|---|---|
| Total overheads allocated (£) | 1,795 | 5,065 |
| Production labour hours | 600 | 1,800 |
| Labour hour rate (£) | 2.99 | 2.81 |

This is an acceptable approach, but it is by no means the only one. Overheads can be charged at a rate per machine hour or as a percentage of the production wages.

However they are charged, this approach will help to ensure that overhead costs are not overlooked when prices are calculated. In order to price a job that is expected to spend two labour hours in department A and one in department B, and which would incur material costs of £200 and wage rate of £6 per hour, it is necessary to carry out the following calculation:

|  | £ |
|---|---|
| Materials | 200 |
| Labour:  A 2 × £6 | 12 |
| B 1 × £6 | 6 |
| Prime or direct cost | 218 |

Add the fixed/overhead cost:

|  |  |
|---|---|
| Department A:  2 × £2.99 | 5.98 |
| Department B:  1 × £2.81 | 2.81 |
|  | 226.79 |

£226.79 is simply the cost of the job. Any profit that was required would have to be added to it. The basis on which the overheads have been allocated with the reasons for the choice are as follows:

- *Rates*. Based on floor area, because this is the usual method of charging rates. Department B has twice the floor area of department A, so the rates are allocated on a basis of two to one: two-thirds of £300 = £200 to department B, and one-third of £300 = £100 to department A.
- *Heating and lighting*. Based on the number of employees, but production labour hours could have been used just as well. Department B has three times as many employees as department A, so heating and lighting are allocated on the basis of three to one: three-quarters of £60 = £45 to department B, and a quarter of £60 = £15 to department A.
- *Depreciation*. Based on the value of machinery. Department A's machinery is four times as valuable as department B's, so depreciation is allocated on the basis of four to one: four-fifths of £100 = £80 goes to department A, and one-fifth of £100 = £20 to department B.
- *Salaries*. Based on the number of labour hours, but the number of employees could have just as easily been used. Department B's production labour hours are three times those of department A, so salaries are allocated on the basis of three to one: three-quarters of £6,000 = £4,500 goes to department B, and one-quarter of £6,000 = £1,500 to department A.
- *Administration*. See if you can calculate this one for yourself and check with the answer given on page 176.

We already have seen that organisations usually have large indirect or overhead costs that are not charged directly to the service or product that is being provided. It is necessary to recover all of these costs if an undertaking is to be seen to be running efficiently or making a profit. Any organisation that employs only the direct costs in arriving at the cost of a service or product will soon cease to exist or else become a drain on the resources of the community.

If, for example, a service organisation provided a simple service and consisted of three departments, it would be possible for it to charge what it considered to be a good rate to its customers and find at the end of the year that it was making a loss. This can be illustrated in the Example 20.

## Example 20

Good Service Ltd has three departments and its expected costs and activity for the next year are:

| | |
|---|---|
| HR department annual fixed costs | £120,000 |
| Finance department annual fixed costs | £100,000 |
| Service department annual fixed costs | £90,000 |
| Service department variable costs | £40 per hour |
| Hours of service to be sold during the year | 5,000 |
| Charge to customers per hour | £100 |

Ignoring the fixed costs of the HR and Finance departments, a charge of £100 per hour seems to be adequate to give a reasonable profit.

| | £ | £ |
|---|---|---|
| Income 5,000 hours at £100 per hour | | 500,000 |
| Expenses | | |
| Fixed costs of Service Department | 90,000 | |
| Variable costs 5,000 hours | | |
| at £40 per hour | 200,000 | |
| | | 290,000 |
| Profit | | 210,000 |

It is only when the costs of the other two departments are considered that it becomes apparent that a loss of £10,000 has been incurred. This is calculated as:

| | £ | £ |
|---|---|---|
| Surplus from Service Department | | 210,000 |
| Less | | |
| Fixed cost of HR Department | 120,000 | |
| Fixed cost of Finance Department | 100,000 | 220,000 |
| Loss | | (10,000) |

In order to avoid this situation it is necessary to find the total charge per hour to ensure that all costs are recovered, together with any profit the company requires. The way to achieve this is first to calculate the charge per hour to recover the fixed costs. That is the total fixed costs divided by the hours of service you expect to sell.

$$\frac{£120,000 + £100,000 + £90,000}{5,000 \text{ hours}} = \frac{£310,000}{5,000 \text{ hours}} = £62 \text{ per hour}$$

If there is to be any profit, this will require an additional cost per hour to the customers. Good Service Ltd requires £40,000 p.a. profit, which necessitates an additional hourly charge of

$$\frac{40,000}{5,000} = £8 \text{ per hour}$$

The charge per hour now becomes

|  | £ |
|---|---|
| Variable cost per hour | 40 |
| *Add* fixed costs per hour | 62 |
| *Add* profit per hour | 8 |
|  | 110 |

The 5,000 hours of service earn: 5,000 × £110 = £550,000

The costs incurred are

| Fixed costs: | £ | £ |
|---|---|---|
| Service Department | 90,000 | |
| HR Department | 120,000 | |
| Finance Department | 100,000 | 310,000 |
| Surplus | | 240,000 |
| *Less* variable cost 5,000 hrs × £40 | | 200,000 |
| Profit | | 40,000 |

In order to explore this a little further let us assume that the total overheads of Poor Real Ltd are £620,000 which are to be allocated to the human resources department, finance department and service department on an equitable basis. There are many ways in which this can be done, including percentage of direct wages, labour hour rate, machine hour rate and number of employees. The number of employees in each of the departments is:

HR department:          15
Service department:     12
Finance department:     13

Using this information to apportion the overheads to the three departments, we share the £620,000 overheads as follows:

HR department          $\dfrac{15}{40}$ x £620,000 = £232,500

Service department     $\dfrac{12}{40}$ x £620,000 = £186,000

Finance department     $\dfrac{13}{40}$ x £620,000 = £201,500

Total as an accuracy check          £620,000

This means that if the organisation is to avoid incurring a loss, the human resources department must earn £232,500, the service department £186,000 and the finance department £201,500; otherwise, as is usually the case, the service department must earn enough to ensure that all the organisation's overheads are recovered.

The apportionment of overheads to departments is a major source of organisational controversy. The human resources manager who unexpectedly finds that the department has had £232,500 overheads charged to it is not going to be at all pleased, particularly as these are costs over which she or he has little or no control. The most effective approach is to tackle the person responsible for the allocation of the overheads and ascertain the basis on which it has been done. You may then be able to challenge the basis on which it has been calculated and argue for a more appropriate figure.

In this chapter we have been considering the traditional absorption methods of allocating overheads, but some people consider that these no longer provide good information for decision-making and control. This concern has encouraged another method of allocating overheads to be developed using cost drivers, called activity-based costing, sometimes referred to as ABC. It is felt to give relevant information to management quickly and so help with decision-making and control. The two methods may be compared diagrammatically in Figures 10 and 11.

This chapter has demonstrated the apportionment of fixed costs to the personnel department, discussed the reasons for controversy over this approach and illustrated the difference between absorption and activity-based costing.

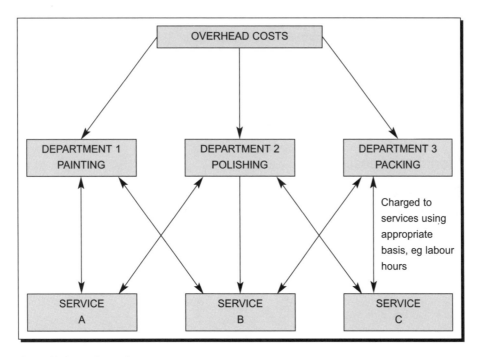

**Figure 10** *Absorption costing*

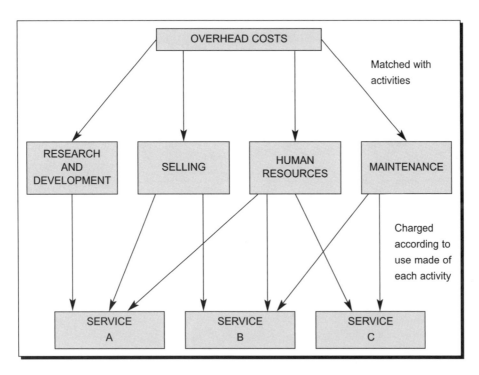

**Figure 11** *Activity-based costing*

## SELF-TEST QUESTIONS

1. What is absorption costing?
2. What is activity-based costing?
3. What is meant by overhead cost apportionment?
4. On what basis would you expect depreciation to be apportioned?
5. Why has activity-based costing been introduced?

## Work-based assignment

Does your department have overhead costs apportioned to it? If so, which system is used, absorption costing or activity-based costing?

# Standard Costing

## OBJECTIVE

At the end of this chapter you will understand the importance of standard costs and the way in which they are set, as well as their use to the human resources manager. The management standard that will be developed is 'managing financial resources to achieve goals and objectives through the budgetary planning and control process'.

Standard costing is extremely important to human resources managers as it can be used to provide a guide to the expected cost of each training programme offered or each member of staff recruited. These can then be compared with the actual costs incurred to help ensure that the department is well managed and that costs are properly controlled. Indeed, the system is critical to the efficiency of the organisation as a whole.

The standard cost is the expected cost per unit, and it is derived from a mixture of historical information and forecasting techniques. The more information that is available, the more accurate the standard is likely to be, but it is important to remember that it is a forecast and will therefore rarely, if ever, be absolutely correct.

Once the standard has been set, it is crucially important to compare the actual result with the expected result, at least monthly but preferably more often, and where they differ significantly to ensure that remedial action is taken promptly.

It is here that a good management information system can be extremely helpful. Most organisations are complex, and people in them receive an enormous amount of information, often in the form of computer printouts. If there are a great number of items that differ from the standard, it will not be possible to correct and report on each one, so two things are necessary.

First, an acceptable difference between the standard and actual results must be decided upon. It will vary from concern to concern but it may be, for example, that anything within + 15 per cent of plan is accepted, whilst anything outside that range has to be reported upon and corrected. Second, the system should then ensure that anything outside the + 15 per cent range is highlighted, perhaps by means of an asterisk, so that the person responsible for correcting the situation is made aware of it and takes the necessary action.

## SETTING STANDARDS

When a standard costing system is established it should be remembered that it has tremendous potential for good or ill. If people feel that it is being foisted upon them without consultation, they will be suspicious and resentful and may cause the system to falter. On the other hand, if they feel that they have been consulted from the beginning and their ideas have been considered, they will feel involved and will want the system to succeed. A sense of ownership is important. In setting the standard or expected cost, too, a great deal of care must be taken. Broadly there are three approaches that are commonly used.

### Perfect standard

This assumes that people in an undertaking can work at peak efficiency throughout the working year. It is, in fact, an impossible target to achieve. The effect on morale is devastating, and eventually the workforce will become totally demotivated, having gone through a cycle from being well motivated and determined to make the system work to disillusioned failure, with their faith in the management of the organisation shattered. Being involved in the discussion, people will work hard to meet the targets, but as they fail to reach them week after week their enthusiasm will wane, until the realisation sets in that it is no good trying because the targets cannot be met and the workforce is totally demoralised.

### Slack standard

This assumes that people do not enjoy being faced with a challenge and would prefer to spend their time talking and doing crosswords than have a demanding job that gives satisfaction through achievement. The target having been set, people will work hard to achieve it, but once they understand that it can be reached week after week with little effort, attention will wander and work will become slipshod. Once again disillusionment will set in as the feeling grows that the organisation neither values its people nor understands their capabilities.

### Standard attainable with effort

This assumes that people become well motivated and will do their best if they are involved in decisions and given tasks that stretch them but can be achieved. In setting the standard, the starting point is past performance. The standards for previous years are studied, and any scope for improvement within achievable limits is built into the standard for the next year. Consultation should take place with the staff responsible for achieving the standard, to obtain their support, and this should help to ensure a well-motivated workforce working to good standards of performance. Where possible, those who consistently achieve above average results should be rewarded in some way, so that people are constantly stimulated to perform well. Realistically, however, it is not always possible to reward good performance in the way that we would like. Much will depend on the culture of the undertaking.

## ELEMENTS OF COST

Costs break down into three elements: labour, materials and overheads, which consist of such items as rates, depreciation and the salaries of 'non-productive' workers. Here 'non-productive' means those who are not directly making the goods or providing the service, and standards have to be set for each of them. The detailed control of overhead costs is outside the scope of this book, and the rest of this chapter will deal with the control of labour and material costs, the ones that can most readily be changed in the short term.

### Labour costs

The expected labour cost of a job or operation can be arrived at by going through the process of reaching an attainable standard (see above). Once it has been set, it is not usually possible to alter a standard very often; in fact it is rarely altered more than once or twice a year. The following illustrations will help to explain the way in which labour costs are controlled, using the labour rate variance and the labour efficiency variance.

- *Labour rate variance*. Caused by changes in rates of pay, and calculated using the formula:

    Actual hours × Change in wage rate per hour

    The change in wage rate per hour is the standard or expected wage rate minus the actual wage rate.
- *Labour efficiency variance*. Caused by changes in the speed of production, and calculated using the formula:

    Standard wage rate per hour × Change in the hours worked

    The change in the hours worked is the standard hours minus the actual hours.

### *Example 21*

The standard cost is four hours at £7 per hour = £28 per unit. The actual cost is:

380 hours at £7.50 per hour = £2,850 per 100 units = £28.50 per unit.

The labour rate variance is (380 × 50p) = £190 adverse.

When costs are greater than the standard, the difference between the budgeted and actual cost is termed an adverse variance. The variance is the difference between the expected and the actual cost, and it is adverse because it is more than expected. Had the cost been less than expected, the variance would have been favourable. It must be emphasised that a favourable variance is as bad as an adverse one, since both indicate a failure to work to plan and may need corrective action. The labour rate variance is adverse because the rate has increased from £7 to £7.50 per hour.

The labour efficiency variance is:

£7(400 – 380) = £140 favourable

The variance is favourable because for 100 units you would expect to use 400 hours but only 380 hours have been used; so the total labour variance is £190 adverse and £140 favourable, which nets down to £50 (£190 – £140) adverse. This can be confirmed by comparing the actual labour cost of £2,850 with the expected labour cost of £2,800 (400 hours at £7 per hour), which confirms the total labour variance of £50 adverse. It therefore shows the calculations of the individual labour variances to be correct.

## Material costs

The process described above for setting an attainable standard, when applied to materials will give the expected material cost of a job or operation, which enables material costs to be controlled through the medium of the material price and material usage variances illustrated below.

- *Material price variance*. Caused by changes in the purchase price of the materials used, and calculated by using the formula:
  Actual quantity × Change in price
  The change in price is the standard minus the actual price.
- *Material usage variance*. Caused by changes in the quantity of materials used, and calculated by using the formula:
  Standard price × Change in use
  The change in use is the standard minus the actual use.

## *Example 22*

The standard material price and usage cost is 20m of material at £8 a metre: £160 per unit. The actual cost is:

2,400m of material at £7.60 a metre    = £18,240 per 100 units
                                                = £182.40 per unit

The material price variance is:

2,400 (£8 – £7.60) = £960 favourable

The material price is favourable because the price has fallen from £8 a metre to £7.60 a metre.

The material usage variance is:

£8 (2,000 – 2,400) = £3,200 adverse

The material usage variance is adverse because the usage has increased from 2,000m to 2,400m.

This enables the total materials variance to be calculated from the £960 favourable variance and the £3,200 adverse variance, giving a net variance of £2,240 adverse. This can be confirmed by comparing the actual material cost of £18,240 with the expected material cost of £16,000 (2,000m × £8 a metre), which confirms the total material variance of £2,240 adverse, and shows the calculation of the individual material variances to be correct.

# CORRECTIVE ACTION

Having calculated the variances and found them to be outside the parameters that are acceptable to the organisation, the information system should flag them in some distinctive way so that the person responsible is made aware that action is necessary. Some possible causes and suggested actions to correct the labour and material variances follow.

## Labour rate variance

1. Bad estimate. Accept as an explainable variance until a new standard can be set.
2. Nationally agreed change in wage rates. Accept until a new standard can be set.
3. Using people who are over- or underskilled for the job. Make the necessary change in the people carrying out the work, and discuss with the supervisor/ manager.

## Labour efficiency variance

1. Bad estimate. Accept until the standard can be changed.
2. Using people who are more or less highly skilled than planned for. Make the necessary changes and have discussions with those responsible.
3. Poor morale among staff. A serious problem for the human resources department, which will have to discover the cause and if possible rectify it; failing all else, people may have to be asked to leave.

## Material price variance

1. Bad estimate. Accept until the standard can be changed.
2. Internationally agreed price change. Accept until the standard can be changed.

3. Using material of a better or worse quality than needed. Make the necessary change in the material used and investigate with the purchasing section.

## Material usage variance

1. Bad estimate. Accept until the standard can be changed.
2. Labour efficiency wastage of material. Explore with the human resources department and correct as quickly as possible.
3. Quality of material. Investigate with purchasing section and take necessary action.
4. People might be taking material to use for their own private purposes.

A good system of standard costing is invaluable to management in helping to ensure that an organisation is adhering to its planned course and things are not getting out of control. The human resources manager who understands costing will not only be better able to control the costs of his or her department and demonstrate its effective management, but will also be able to assist in other areas, especially where variances in labour costs can be attributed to a mismatch between people's skills and their functions.

This chapter has discussed standard costing and its application to human resources, as well as the ways in which standards are set and the limitations of each.

Work through Exercises 13–15 and compare your answers with the suggested ones given at the back of the book.

## Exercise 13

A service organisation has the following standard costs per day for the service it provides: labour, 8 hours at £40 per hour; materials, 5 litres at £15 per litre; overheads, £60 per day. The actual costs for one week of five days are: labour, 38 hours at £41 per hour; materials, 28 litres at £14.50 per litre; overheads, £340. Calculate the variances and comment on their use.

## Exercise 14

The human resources department is responsible for providing a one-week 40-hour induction programme for new recruits. The standard costs of the programme are: hourly salary per recruit, £7.20; hourly salary per trainer, £8.65; overhead costs per week for the personnel department, £1,000. The actual costs of a training week for 20 delegates are:

| | £ |
|---|---|
| 42 hours training for 20 delegates with salaries of £7 per hour | 5880.00 |
| 42 hours training by 2 trainers with salaries of £8.70 per hour | 730.80 |
| Overheads | 1200.00 |
| | 7810.80 |

Calculate the relevant variances and comment on their use to the human resources manager.

## Exercise 15

Explain the main factors of standard costing that make it an effective control tool for human resources managers.

## SELF-TEST QUESTIONS

1. How are standard costs set?
2. What is a favourable variance?
3. What is the effect of a perfect standard on staff?
4. Why is it important to take corrective action when variances occur?

## Work-based assignment

How could standard costing be used by the human resources manager to motivate staff in your organisation?

# Marginal Costing and Human Resource Decisions

## CHAPTER 13

## OBJECTIVE

At the end of this chapter you will be able to employ marginal costing in decision-making and understand its use to the human resources manager. The management standards that will be developed are 'managing financial resources to achieve goals and objectives through the budgetary planning and control process', 'interpreting information from key financial statements' and 'analysing financial and other information used in making outsourcing decisions.'

We have so far been concerned with ensuring that all costs are accounted for and recovered. There is also an approach to costing that focuses attention on those costs that will be altered by a particular decision, in order to emphasise the impact of the decision. This approach is called marginal costing, and whilst it is not a complete system it is of enormous help to the human resources manager when making decisions, for example about selling training or consultancy services (whether within or outside the organisation).

Under marginal costing the fixed costs, such as depreciation, salaries and interest charges, are considered to have been set as a matter of policy and to remain fixed within given parameters for the period under review. This is not to say that the fixed costs are not important. For most undertakings they contribute the bulk of the costs incurred and to ignore them completely would be a recipe for disaster. But they can be regarded as not directly affecting a decision that is being made. The marginal cost can be described as the cost of one more unit, be it a product or a service, and the difference between these two costs can be graphically illustrated in Figures 12 and 13.

The marginal cost line starts at zero because if nothing is being done – no service provided or units made – no marginal cost is being incurred, whereas the fixed cost line is parallel to the base because the cost is the same whether one unit or eight units of product or service is being provided.

Marginal costing employs the important concept of contribution. Contribution is the selling price per unit of service or product minus the marginal cost per unit of providing it. The contribution goes first towards meeting the fixed costs of the organisation and then, provided the contribution is large enough, it becomes profit. If the contribution is not enough to meet the fixed costs a loss is incurred, as can be seen in the following illustration.

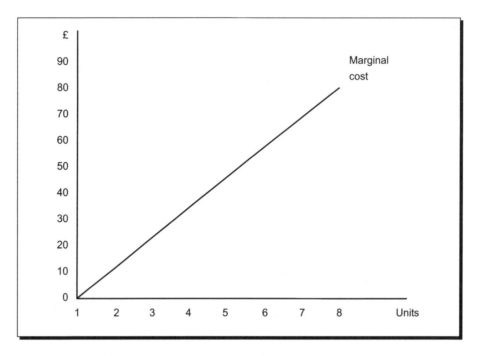

**Figure 12** *Marginal costs*

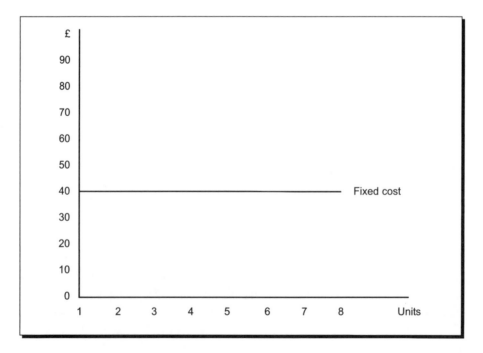

**Figure 13** *Fixed costs*

# Example 23

The human resources department offers training, for which it charges £100 per hour, for up to 20 delegates. The marginal costs have been calculated at £70 per hour and the fixed costs for the period are £9,990. The manager needs to know the contribution per hour, how many hours of training must be sold to break even (ie make neither a profit nor a loss), and what the profit or loss would be if 350 hours of training were sold.

The contribution per hour is the selling price per hour minus the marginal cost per hour:

£100 – £70 = £30

The number of hours that must be sold in order to break even is:

$$\frac{\text{Fixed costs}}{\text{Contribution per hour}} = \frac{£9,990}{£30} = 333 \text{ hours}$$

The profit or loss if 350 hours of training are sold is the total contribution minus the fixed costs:

£10,500 (£30 × 350 hours) – 9,990 = £510

Let us look at another example of how this concept is used.

# Example 24

A human resources consultancy organisation has fixed costs of £60,000, marginal costs of £50 per unit and a selling price of £150 per unit. Each unit that is sold contributes £100 to the fixed costs, and once these have been met the contribution is to profit. This can be further illustrated as shown in the table.

| Units sold | Contribution (£) | Fixed costs (£) | Profit (or loss)(£) |
|---|---|---|---|
| 0 | 0 | 60,000 | (60,000) |
| 1 | 100 | 60,000 | (59,900) |
| 2 | 200 | 60,000 | (59,800) |
| 3 | 300 | 60,000 | (59,700) |
| 599 | 59,900 | 60,000 | (100) |
| 600 | 60,000 | 60,000 | (0) break even |
| 601 | 60,100 | 60,000 | 100 |

At 600 units the organisation breaks even. More than 600 units results in a profit, and less in a loss. The break-even point in units sold can be calculated by applying the formula:

$$\frac{\text{Total fixed costs}}{\text{Selling price} - \text{marginal cost per unit}}$$

which in our example gives:

$$\frac{60,000}{(150 - 50)} = \frac{60,000}{100} = 600 \text{ units}$$

The relationship may be shown graphically (see Figure 14) if we assume the information previously given applies and the maximum possible number units that can be sold is 700.

The horizontal axis represents activity, in this case the units sold, and the vertical axis value in terms of both costs and revenue. The horizontal axis goes to the maximum possible level of activity, and at this point a vertical line is drawn, which shows where all the lines of the graph end. The vertical axis must go up to the total sales or the total

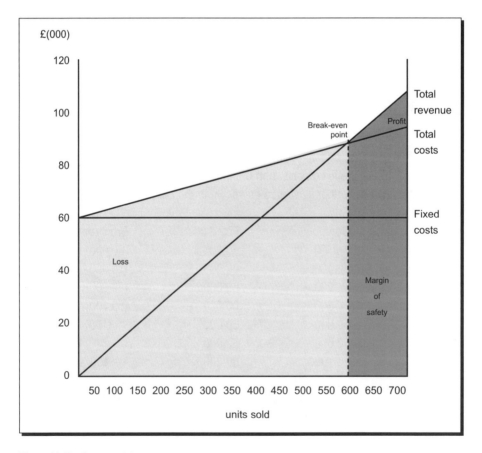

**Figure 14** *Break-even point*

costs, whichever is the greater. The total revenue is obtained by multiplying the total units sold by the selling price per unit

$700 \times 150 = £105,000$

A mark is made on the vertical line opposite the £105,000. This is then joined to the zero to give the total revenue line. The total cost is calculated by adding the fixed cost to the total marginal cost, which in this case is:

(marginal cost per unit $\times$ units sold) + fixed costs = (£50 $\times$ 700) + £60,000 = £35,000 + £60,000 = £95,000

A mark is made on the vertical axis opposite the £95,000 and joined to the fixed costs of £60,000 to give the total cost line. The break-even point is where the total cost and total revenue lines intercept. Anything to the left of it represents loss; anything to the right of it, profit.

Contribution is used by many organisations in an attempt to ensure that spare capacity is fully employed at off-peak times. Rail and bus companies, British Telecom, the electricity undertakings, British Airways and hotel chains are among those that have high fixed costs and employ a two-tier or multi-tier pricing system in order to persuade the public to use their services at off-peak times. Every extra contribution that is received helps to meet the enormous fixed costs they carry and either reduces losses or increases profits. Full rates are charged at peak periods but at off-peak times bargain offers are made. For example, National Rail charges approximately £49 return from Portsmouth to Waterloo at peak times, but reduces it to £26 at other periods. Provided they are receiving more in fares than it is costing to run the train, they are receiving a contribution to their enormous fixed costs.

We have seen that there are several costing methods available to the human resources manager. The one you choose should meet your needs and provide you with relevant information to manage yourself and your department more effectively. Decisions based on incomplete or inappropriate information are bad decisions. To be successful, it is essential to have the right information in the right place at the right time.

This chapter has explained marginal costing and its use to human resource managers as an aid to decision-making. It emphasised the importance of marginal costs while reminding us that fixed costs are ignored at the peril of the department or organisation concerned.

## Exercise 16

Look at Example 23. What would you recommend should be done if demand for training fell to 300 hours? What would be the magnitude of the loss?

## Exercise 17

The human resources department markets its services in recruitment consultancy. The marginal cost has been calculated to be £19,500 per managerial appointment and the charge to the customers is £25,000 per appointment. The relevant fixed costs are £319,000 and it is expected that 70 managerial recruitments will be undertaken for clients. Draw the break-even chart for the above information, and read from the chart the results of the planned 70 recruits.

## Exercise 18

Enumerate three ways in which the concept of contribution is of help to human resource managers.

## Exercise 19

Your Managing Director is reviewing training costs with a view to possibly purchasing training from consultants rather than employing your department. The costs of buying in training for the standard induction programme would be £4,000 for up to 20 delegates. The costs charged by your department are £6,000 for up to 20 delegates. The overheads charged to the department from head office are £10,000 and they are recovered in the quoted costs over four programmes.

How would you demonstrate to the Managing Director that your department's costs are lower than those of the outside consultant?

## Exercise 20

The human resources department is selling its training services to outside organisations. It charges £400 per hour for up to 30 delegates. The marginal cost is known to be £200 per hour and the relevant fixed costs are £30,000.

There is currently demand for 200 hours of training. Using the above information:

1. Draw the break-even chart.
2. Calculate the contribution per hour.
3. What is the break-even number of hours sold?
4. What would the profit or loss be if 300 hours of training were sold?
5. What would the profit or loss be if demand for training fell to 100 hours?

# Exercise 21

Using the information provided in Exercise 20, your manager has calculated that if the charge per hour was reduced to £300 demand would increase to 550 hours and has asked for your advice as to whether or not the proposed changes should be made. State, giving reasons, what you would recommend.

Questions

1. Draw a break-even chart assuming the maximum demand to be 300 hours.
2. What is the contribution per hour?
3. What is the break-even point in hours sold?
4. What profit is being made or loss incurred?
5. What would be the profit or loss if demand fell to 100 hours?

## SELF-TEST QUESTIONS

1. What is the marginal cost?
2. How is contribution calculated?
3. What are fixed costs?
4. How is the break-even point calculated?

## Work-based assignment

Investigate the application of marginal costing to the human resources function in your organisation.

# Budgets and Human Behaviour

## CHAPTER 14

## OBJECTIVE

At the end of this chapter the reader should understand the effect that the budgetary control system has on the behaviour of people in organisations.

Research has demonstrated that organisations would like the people in them to behave in ways that benefit the organisation and avoid actions that would improve the employee's quality of life at the organisation's expense. In an ideal world the goals of the firm and the individual would be the same but unfortunately this rarely if ever happens except in the case of the sole trader. The undertaking would like efficient employees who work hard for its benefit for the whole working day throughout the year. Employees are certainly prepared to work hard for the organisation but they also put value on quality of life, which means that they have interests that do not necessarily meet those of the employers. Management might prefer to be on the golf course rather than attending a planning meeting. Team members might prefer attending a rugby match to selling services or products. It is here that the human resources manager can be of value in devising ways in which people's behaviour can be modified to more closely meet the needs of the organisation.

We know that money is a great motivator, but at some stage a point is reached at which individuals reach saturation and would rather be relaxing and following a favoured hobby than earning more money. To help them concentrate on organisational needs, other forms of incentive have to be devised. Performance-related pay works up to a point, but what then? A larger office, a bigger piece of carpet, a holiday on the chief executive's yacht, a trip overseas, a new job title, congratulations on an outstanding performance published in the monthly newsletter, a presentation of a gold pen and pencil set by the chief executive or a new job title –all these have been tried with some success in the past. The problem for the human resources manager is to decide which scheme or combination of schemes is most appropriate for the organisation in question. Many incentives are more easily applied in the private than the public sector because of the restrictions under which the public sector has to operate. That is not meant to suggest that the private sector operates in an easier environment than the public sector because they both work in a highly competitive arena, but they are differently regulated and the private firm has a little more freedom of action.

Whatever the human resources manager decides to do there has to be some means of identifying the people who should be rewarded for a job well done, not only as a reward for those individuals but also as an incentive for others to emulate them. It is here that a good system of budgetary control can provide invaluable help in providing targets against which performance can be measured. We have already seen that good goal setting is absolutely critical to the motivation or otherwise of the people involved. Past research has shown that organisations that impose targets from above receive less cooperation than those that set targets only after consultation with staff that will have to make the scheme work. The advice they give does not have to be followed for people to feel greater motivation; rather, the fact that they have been consulted gives them a sense of ownership and worth. Even here one has to be careful, because some staff feel that it is the job of the 'management' to run the organisation and that they are not paid to advise the bosses. It used to be thought that if staff were allowed to set their own targets they would build in slack in order to make life easier for themselves, but this has not proved to be the case. When people have been made responsible, they have set targets that stretch and challenge them enough to make life interesting. It is as dangerous to underestimate staff motivation as it is to overestimate it.

Budgetary control is of great assistance to management when employed effectively; it provides a means of persuading people to behave in a manner that benefits the organisation. There are major problems and the human resources manager can be of great assistance in helping to overcome them. The manager must ensure that staff feel they are valued by the organisation and that they are working in an environment that meets their needs. Each undertaking has its own culture and attempts to employ people it feels will fit into that culture without being too disruptive, whilst recruited staff need to feel accepted by their peers and comfortable in their new surroundings. The costs of a poor recruitment decision are enormous both to the organisation and to the individual involved. The undertaking is concerned because there will be major disruption to the working of the team and/or department within which the new person works if it transpires that a poor decision has been made. This will have a knock-on effect throughout the undertaking. On top of this there will be the costs involved in retraining and development of the individual, and at worst there will be major disciplinary procedures followed by fresh recruitment costs. This could also have a detrimental impact on the reputation of the organisation in the market place, and the whole experience may destroy the confidence of the person involved.

The above scenario shows that it is absolutely critical for the human resources manager and the undertaking to ensure that the right procedures are in place to recruit, develop, motivate and retain good staff. To achieve this each member of the team must know exactly what is expected of him or her as well as what constitutes unacceptable, acceptable, good and outstanding levels of performance. It is here that a well-developed system of planning and control can be invaluable in providing a yardstick against which achievement can be measured. Despite some of the theories that have been tested in schools in the United Kingdom over the last 30 years or so, people are naturally competitive and respond favourably to a challenge so long as it is set within their capacity to meet it. We have already seen that it is of little or no use to set a plan for a year, then look at it again 12 months later only to say 'oh dear it did not work out as we had hoped'. For it to work from a motivational as well as a control aspect, there must be a continuous monitoring of actual against planned performance levels so that people can be encouraged and any necessary corrective action taken early enough to be effective. People will modify their behaviour so that they maximise their personal satisfaction as well as their material reward, which will also benefit the employing undertaking, making it more effective in the environment in which it operates.

Budgetary control can and does persuade people to modify their behaviour in ways that are of benefit to all concerned. For example, if there were no financial plan for human resources in your organisation the staff would take a laissez-faire approach and would not be at all concerned about what was spent or when it was spent – that is until money ran out and the department or section was no longer able to operate. The introduction of budgetary control would have an immediate impact on staff behaviour in that they would be aware of the financial resources that were available and would take the action necessary to ensure money was spent at the right time and on agreed items. There would be even more reason for people to modify their approach if some sort of incentive scheme reinforced the system so that people were rewarded for behaving as the organisation wanted. This does not apply to human resources alone but to the whole undertaking, irrespective of whether it is in the public or private sector. A local authority that took 250 elderly people into its care homes and then had to expel 50 of them half way through the year because it was running out of money would be pilloried by the media and might well find itself subject to government investigation so that its very existence would be in jeopardy. Good planning and control would help ensure that staff were motivated to avoid such an outcome by monitoring actual expenditures and comparing them with the plan so as to enable them to take any necessary remedial action in good time. A computer manufacturer that took orders for 5,000 computers when it only had sufficient resources to make 2,000 would find that it had lost customers as well as credibility in the market, which could well put it out of business. This could again be avoided by a good system of budgetary control that would provide the basis for well-motivated staff to make estimates on good information that were realistic and manageable.

In conclusion we can see that a good system of budgetary control helps motivate staff to work effectively for the benefit of the undertaking, and by so doing improves their job satisfaction as well as their quality of life. Organisations that have no system of budgetary control may survive but they certainly will not prosper, because staff will be in the unhappy position of not knowing what is expected of them and will therefore lack motivation. How would you feel if you worked in a structure that was so lacking in direction that no one was in a position to congratulate you at the end of a year in which you had worked extremely hard? All that would be required to improve the situation is a set of targets against which you could be measured. This would enable your performance to be assessed and praised where appropriate, thus improving your motivation and sense of well-being.

## SELF-TEST QUESTIONS

1. What is the purpose of budgetary control?
2. How does budgetary control affect the behaviour of people?
3. Does budgetary control apply to both the public and private sectors?
4. How does budgetary control help motivate staff?

## Work-based assignment

What is the impact of budgetary control in your organisation?

# The Human Resources Manager and the Planning System

## OBJECTIVE

At the end of this chapter you will understand the planning process and its application to the organisation as well as to the human resources department. The management standards that will be developed are 'managing financial resources to achieve goals and objectives through the budgetary planning and control process' and 'evaluating business plans for functional organisational projects'.

A chart of the planning system is shown in Figure 15. In following this model we see that the first purpose of the planning system is to ensure that organisational objectives are set. This is usually undertaken by the top executives, normally including the chief executive together with his or her deputy, the human resources director, financial director and marketing director. Other people may be co-opted onto the team as they are required but it is usual to keep the group to a workable size whenever possible. In setting the objectives the team will have regard to the past performance of the organisation, particularly over the last two or three years, as well as the likely events of the next five years or so which will have an impact on it. In doing this they will consider reports from people who are in touch with the customers, so that any changes in customer profile can be quickly identified. The latest economic forecasts will be considered, together with population trends and expected changes in fashion and technology. There are a great many different organisational objectives that might be set, including such things as providing the fastest service, being most concerned about the environment, having the largest market share, having the happiest employees, making the biggest profit or making the most reliable product. Organisations like The Body Shop set great store on being environmentally friendly and in view of the perceived threat from global warming this approach is attracting huge support. At the same time oil producing firms are being vilified because of their apparent lack of concern for the environment.

The objectives may be for up to 10 years ahead, but it is important to remember that they are subject to change. No undertaking survives for long in the current highly competitive environment unless it is able to respond quickly and effectively to changing conditions, but objectives do set a course that the organisation is able to follow.

The planning process is a long iterative procedure that cannot be completed in a day, a week, a month or usually even a year. The more often an organisation undertakes

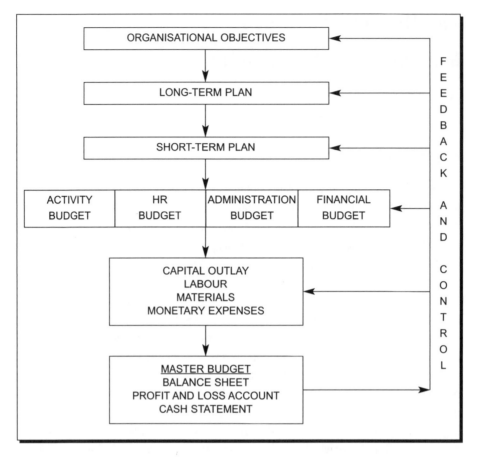

**Figure 15** *The planning system*

the planning process the easier it becomes and there is no doubt that first attempts can be an extremely chastening but rewarding experience, both for those involved and the organisation itself.

## THE LONG-RANGE PLAN

This is drawn up to enable the objectives to be achieved and will probably cover the next 10 years, but it is important to remember that it is virtually impossible to plan accurately so far into the future. The first year will be relatively firm, and years 2–3 should be fairly accurate unless something unexpected occurs, like the bursting of the technology bubble in 2000 and the subsequent collapse of the stock market from which it has yet to fully recover.

Years 4 and 5 will be rather less certain, and years 6–10 pretty tentative, except perhaps in the case of large projects that require extensive capital outlay. The long-range plan will be adjusted year by year as a result of feedback as to its feasibility, once it has been expressed in financial terms in the master budget. The long-range plan, and in particular the early years of it, will see a great deal of in-fighting as each manager stakes a claim to as large a share of the budget 'cake' as possible. Personalities will be very much to the fore, and there is a real danger that, unless there is a good system with a reasonable approach, the most aggressive character will receive far more than his or her entitlement. It is important that the human resources manager should make a good case, otherwise the department will suffer.

## THE SHORT-RANGE PLAN

This will be the budget for the next 12 months, and before it is finished consultation will ideally have taken place at all levels of the concern. Without the opportunity to be involved in the preparation of the budget, people will feel that it has been imposed on them and be resentful. If, on the other hand, they feel that they have contributed to its preparation they are more likely to feel involved and supportive, so that the chances of the plan being adhered to will be greatly enhanced.

The budget works in the same way as standard costing, the difference being in scale. Whereas standard costing refers to a job, operation, section or department, budgetary control encompasses the whole organisation, but uses exactly the same technique as standard costing. Actual performance is compared with planned performances on a weekly, monthly or quarterly basis, and significant differences are reported upon so that corrective action can be taken. The behavioural impact of the system is extremely important as it can have a major effect on the way people behave.

## THE BUDGETS

The short-range plan feeds into the detailed budgets discussed below, which are firm for the first year but become more tentative the further they go into the future. With all planning it is important to be flexible and to allow for the unexpected, as things will change; attempts to treat a budget as set in tablets of stone, under no circumstances to be altered, will cause more problems than they solve. Even under these conditions it is better to plan than attempt to fly purely by the 'seat of your pants' – a sure recipe for disaster.

### Activity budget

This consists of the expected hours of service that an organisation believes it can provide in the period that is being planned for, or units it can produce, or jobs it can complete. It will be based on the information – provided by market research carried out by the undertaking's employees or bought in – as to the likely level of demand. The information will have to be handled with care, as there is a danger that people will want to paint an optimistic picture and may unintentionally overstate the level of demand. To help counteract this, it is a good idea to obtain information from as many sources as possible and to prepare three levels of activity, most pessimistic, most optimistic and most likely. This will help to minimise the risk of people getting carried away with their own enthusiasm.

Having set the budget, it is essential to monitor it closely to ensure that errors are quickly noticed and the relevant corrections made. Bad planning here will have an impact throughout the whole concern, as will be discussed later in this chapter.

## Human resources budget

In order to meet the level of demand anticipated by the activity budget, it is essential to ensure that enough people of the right calibre are available throughout the organisation. To achieve this, effective recruitment systems have to be in place, reinforced by job analysis and training programmes. It is fashionable and necessary for both the public and private sectors to be lean and healthy, and for them to succeed the people must operate effectively.

The fast-changing environment in which we all operate means that people must be flexible in their approach and constantly retrained to keep up with current developments. The human resource manager has a key role in ensuring that the requirements of staff for development are identified and met. Failure to achieve this will lead first to a demotivated team, because staff will feel that they are not performing effectively, and then to the possible demise of the organisation as it fails to compete with more efficient concerns.

## Administration budget

Built around the expected level of activity, this budget will ensure that the correct administrative systems are in place with suitably experienced and/or qualified people to enable the organisation to meet the demands that are placed upon it. Obtaining the right person to meet the particular needs of a section or department is an extremely specialised matter, and recruitment consultants are frequently called in, particularly for the more senior positions. Good administration can help ensure the successful implementation of plans, so this budget should be capable of providing the necessary resources to meet the concern's needs.

## Financial budget

The financial budget is based on the activity budget, and is used to ensure that there are sufficient financial resources for the plan to be met. Undertakings need resources of materials, labour and money to enable them to operate, and a shortage of any one of these will cause plans to fail. Finance is used in every area, as are people and materials, but there is a danger that the financial implications of plans or actions may sometimes be overlooked. The preparation of the financial budget helps to ensure that this does not happen, as every manager is involved and the accountant's role, contrary to popular belief, is simply to clothe the managers' ideas in monetary terms. If this process is not carried out effectively there is a high chance of failure, as has been the case with MG Rover Group, which for a variety of reasons ran out of money.

In the past some accountants have been seen as unapproachable people, speaking a strange language, whose main purpose in life was to say 'no', and whose second great desire was to confuse. This is now changing and the accountant is seen more as an organisational resource, a person who can give valuable advice on a great many matters.

## Capital outlay budget

Capital outlay involves heavy expenditure on such fixed assets as land and buildings, plant and machinery, or fixtures and fittings, which may be spent in one year but may also involve large capital programmes spread over several years. Examples would be a new housing estate, a land reclamation scheme, a drainage system, a sports complex, the development of a commercial dock or the rebuilding of Wembley Stadium, which is due to be completed in March 2006. The capital budget, unlike the revenue budgets, often involves heavy expenditure spread over several years and should therefore receive close scrutiny before any schemes are finally approved. Various methods are available and they are described in Chapter 17.

## Materials budget

This is prepared in order to ensure that sufficient materials are available to meet the anticipated demand, whilst at the same time enabling the undertaking to avoid tying up too much money in unnecessarily high stocks of material. The level will depend on the forecasts in the activity budget, but it should be borne in mind that more and more organisations are attempting to use the 'just in time' method of inventory control. In practice this is extremely difficult to achieve, as so much depends on the reliability of the supplier, with any small delay causing enormous problems.

## Cash budget

This is a more sensitive version of the financial budget; it concentrates on the day-to-day movements of money in the concern. It is complementary to the financial budget, and draws on the activity and other budgets. Properly monitored, the cash budget can be extremely helpful in controlling the activities of the organisation and avoiding embarrassing short-term cash-flow problems. As mentioned earlier, many chief executives ensure that surplus cash is invested on the money market overnight to earn interest. The cash budget is dealt with in Chapter 16.

## Expenses budget

This covers the expected level of such items of expense as rates, heating and lighting, telephones, postage, stationery and canteen costs. Most of them will be known with a reasonable degree of certainty, at least for the next year, and, whilst they have to be integrated with the other budgets, they are not so directly changed by differing levels of activity.

## Master budget

The master budget clothes these ideas in monetary terms to see whether they are in fact feasible when measured against planned levels of profitability and liquidity. If it shows that there will be a loss instead of a profit, or that too little money will be generated, the information will be fed back into the system and the process restarted.

None of the budgets mentioned can stand on its own, and each depends on the others. It is no use planning to provide 10,000 hours of service if you only have enough people to give 7,000, or to produce 50,000 units if you are only able to sell 40,000. To avoid mismatching of this sort, organisations have to decide what their limiting factor is: that is to say, which of the budgets is most restricted, either through shortage of resources or because of a lack of demand. Once identified, the limiting factor becomes the starting point of the budget, and all the others are built around it. An undertaking may decide that it can meet any level of demand, and if this is so, then the activity or sales budget will be the starting point and all the other budgets will be dependent on it, as illustrated in Figure 16. This shows an integrated system of budgeting in which each budget has an impact on the others, but the one that restricts the overall budgets – in this case is the activity/sales budget, as the concern feels that, whatever the demand, it has the resources to meet it – is used as the starting point.

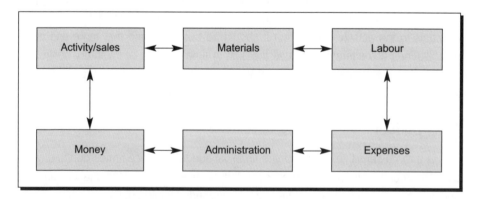

**Figure 16** *Limiting factor activity/sales budget*

The system is as appropriate for the public sector as it is for the private sector, but the limiting factor in the public sector is frequently money and so the model would be as in Figure 17.

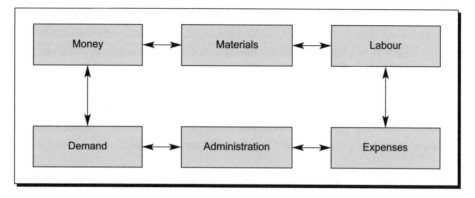

**Figure 17** *Limiting factor cash budget*

## APPROACHES TO BUDGETING

We have seen that the preparation of the budget is an extremely time consuming process that involves people throughout the organisation but we have considered only one approach. Two others that are often employed are 'flexible budgeting' and 'zero-based budgeting' which employ the same principles as we have already discussed but use different approaches. The traditional approach looks at what has happened in the past and then adjusts the levels of future activity to take account of anticipated changes. It assumes that what the organisation has been doing in the past is correct and necessary for future success. This is not always the case and often things are wrongly continued simply because they have been happening and nobody has scrutinised them very closely for some years. Zero-based budgeting helps to overcome this problem because it requires every activity centre and budget head to justify each item of income and expenditure without any recourse to the past. It questions each activity and assumes that none of them has the right to exist; rather, all departments have to justify their actions to the organisation. This approach is much more time consuming than the traditional one because so much detail is required, but it has the advantage that it helps to eliminate waste and inefficiency. Zero-based budgeting (sometimes termed ZBB) originated in military organisations in the United States and has been quite widely adopted there. It has not been so popular in the United Kingdom because it is time consuming and expensive. Some public sector organisations employ it, and others use it once every five years or so to help ensure only essential tasks are undertaken and to give people a better understanding of their roles.

Flexible budgeting takes account of the impact of different levels of activity on the budget before attempting to exercise control by comparing actual expenditure or income with the expected level. If demand for the goods or services provided by an undertaking were to increase or decrease by 200 per cent it would have a dramatic impact on income as well as expenditure. This would mean that when the original budget was compared with the actual figures there would be some huge differences (variances) that would have to be explained. In order to overcome this problem the accountant will change or 'flex' the budget to take account of the new circumstances, making sure that only budget headings affected by the change in activity are amended. Generally speaking the variable costs would be altered but the fixed costs would remain unchanged. This approach is widely employed in the United Kingdom, but the flexing is usually carried out after the change has occurred rather than going through the time-consuming process of preparing a flexible budget for 16 or more levels of activity with no guarantee that the right one had been chosen.

Budgeting, like any other human activity, requires a set of target dates if it is to happen quickly enough to be useful. It is for this reason that the budget timetable is prepared and given to each manager with responsibility for providing information that is needed for the satisfactory completion of the budget. The timing will vary from undertaking to undertaking, but it might for example require departmental managers to provide their plans to the budget committee by 31 July. Draft budget meeting 30 October, revised budget meeting 31 January, final budget meeting 31 March. Final budget produced 31 May for financial year commencing 1 September. The process is so critical that it has to be closely monitored to ensure that no slippage takes place. A manager who does not know the departmental budget at the start of the financial year is a demotivated manager who will not remain at the organisation long, and the organisation itself will be at risk of failure. The human resources manager can play a key role here in helping to ensure that people understand what is required of them and remain motivated to meet critical dates.

This chapter has explained the planning process and the critical part it plays in helping to ensure that organisations fulfil their potential. It has also illustrated the need for human resources to plan to enable their department to contribute fully to the success of the organisation.

## Exercise 22

An organisation has budgeted sales for three months (12 weeks) of 600 units at £20 each. The material bought and used will be 300 lb at 60p a pound. The labour cost will be 360 hours at £15 per hour, and other expenses £40 per week. The cash in hand at the start of the period is £400. Customers receive one month's credit, and suppliers and other expenses are paid on time. Draw up the sales, materials, labour, expenses and cash budgets for the three months, and the budgeted profit and loss account and balance sheet. No money was due from customers. At the beginning of the three months, there was 10lb of material in hand and £406 capital.

## Exercise 23

The following information has been prepared for Bard limited for the year ending 31 December 2005.

| | Budget | Actual |
|---|---|---|
| Activity level | 50% | 60% |
| | £ | £ |
| Costs | | |
| Direct materials | 100,000 | 122,000 |
| Direct labour | 200,000 | 236,000 |
| Variable overhead | 20,000 | 28,000 |
| Total variable cost | 320,000 | 386,000 |
| Fixed overhead | 80,000 | 84,000 |
| Total costs | 400,000 | 470,000 |

Required: prepare a flexed budget for Bard limited for the year ending 31 December 2005.

## Exercise 24

Using the following information, produce a cash budget for Personnel Ltd for the six months ended 30 June 2005:

| | Jan £'000 | Feb £'000 | March £'000 | April £'000 | May £'000 | June £'000 |
|---|---|---|---|---|---|---|
| Receipts from customers | 240 | 1,200 | 1,600 | 800 | 1,400 | 1,800 |
| Payments; | | | | | | |
| Materials | 100 | 400 | 600 | 400 | 1,000 | 200 |
| Wages | 440 | 480 | 500 | 500 | 550 | 580 |
| Overhead expenses | 60 | 50 | 50 | 60 | 70 | 80 |

The cash in hand on 1 January 2005 was £100,000

## SELF-TEST QUESTIONS

1. What is the limiting factor?
2. How does the planning system impact people's behaviour?
3. Why should the human resources manager be involved in the process?
4. Why is the budget timetable important?

## Work-based assignment

Prepare a model of your organisation's planning system and compare it with the one illustrated in this chapter. What do you consider to be its strengths and weaknesses? What is the human resources manager's contribution to the planning system? Identify the main items of income and expenditure for which she or he is responsible.

Draw up the plan or budget for the human resources department for the coming year. If you do not know how much money will be involved for each item, simply list the headings involved.

# The Master Budget

## OBJECTIVE

At the end of this chapter you will understand the preparation of the master budget and its links with the other budgets of the concern. The management standards that will be developed are 'managing financial resources to achieve goals and objectives through the budgetary planning and control process', 'interpreting information from key financial statements', 'evaluating business plans for functional organisational projects', 'critically appraising proposals for capital projects', 'analysing financial and other information used in making outsourcing decisions' and 'evaluating the financial implications of sustainable development.'

The master budget consists of the forecast trading and profit and loss account, revenue account, balance sheet and cash statement. It draws on all the other budgets and can be completed only after they have been prepared. The budgeting process is a long-drawn-out affair which takes up to nine months, and there are usually several attempts before the plan is finally agreed. There is a danger that people will become cynical about the process because they may have observed over the years, for example, that, whatever is set as the first budget is returned with a request that it should be pruned by 15 per cent. This makes them inflate the original plan by 15 per cent in the expectation that when the negotiations are completed they will receive the budget allocation they feel is necessary to allow them to function effectively.

Most budgets are set by looking at what has happened in the past and then adding whatever is necessary to keep up with inflation and extra needs. This has the adverse effect of making people spend up to budget in the last month of two of a year, as they fear that any unspent money will be lost and as a consequence the budget for the next year will be reduced. Zero-based budgeting has been introduced as a means of avoiding this. This approach looks at the future needs of each budget centre and ignores anything that has happened in the past. The budget centre – which may be a branch, a department, a section or a product – is asked to submit its plan, and this is compared with requests from all the other budget centres before a decision is made. It is believed that this avoids the rush to spend up to budget before the year's end and so saves money, although it is a more time consuming approach.

This process of negotiation means that the master budget has to be revised several times before the process is complete, because the original plans may lead to a shortage of cash or a loss instead of a profit, and this information will be fed back into the system as illustrated on page 128, allowing the necessary revisions to be made. The master budget allows the results of the planned activities to be expressed in the international language of money, and provides a concise overall picture of the situation that can be readily assimilated and discussed by those concerned.

We have already seen that the budget for the human resources department is an integral part of this process. The human resources manager will have consulted with his or her staff to ascertain the likely level of activity over the forthcoming year for all aspects of the department's functions. Ideally these plans will be fully discussed within the department before they are finally submitted to the budget committee. If the department is to function effectively, it is essential for all members to be fully committed to its objectives as stated in the budget, and the best way to obtain this commitment is through involvement – ownership is important.

Different departmental managers have different approaches to the process and a great deal depends on the character of the individual involved. There is a danger in constantly asking for more or less than you require to run your department effectively, in that you may well lose the respect of your colleagues. The manager who in the long term gains most from the negotiations is the one who makes careful estimates of future activities based on the information available at the time. There will of course be mistakes but as long as they are seen and corrected early enough no major damage will be done.

Let us now consider the master budget of a manufacturing concern. The process followed is that illustrated in the model system in Chapter 15. We will first show the budget and the relationships between the figures and the budgets from which they have been derived. This will be followed by the budget of a public authority (Example 26).

## Example 25

The tables give the accounts of 'Makes Co.' for the year ending 30 June. From these examples it can be seen that the budgetary control system is totally integrated, and can be of use to the organisation only as long as it remains so. If any one budget endeavours to stand on its own, the system becomes useless. The way in which the budget is drawn up from basic information is shown in the previous chapter, which should be further studied in conjunction with this chapter.

We have already seen that the master budget is drawn up after all the other budgets have been prepared. One of these, the cash budget, is vital to organisational survival. It is because of this that we will now consider it in greater detail.

*Example 25a*
### Forecast manufacturing accounts of 'Makes Co.' for the year ending 30 June

| | £ | £ |
|---|---|---|
| Opening inventory of raw materials | | 40,000 |
| *Add* raw materials purchased | | 810,000 |
| | | 850,000 |
| *Deduct* closing inventory of raw materials | | 60,000 |
| | | 790,000 |
| Raw materials consumed | | 1,410,000 |
| Direct manufacturing wages | | 10,000 |
| Direct expenses | | |
| | | 2,210,000 |
| Prime/direct cost of goods made | | |
| | | |
| *Add* Indirect factory expenses/overheads: | | |
| Salaries and wages | 70,000 | |
| Materials | 30,000 | |
| Heating and lighting | 40,000 | |
| Rent and rates | 60,000 | |
| Depreciation | 90,000 | |
| Total manufacturing cost | | 290,000 |
| *Add* opening work in progress | | 2,500,000 |
| *Deduct* closing work in progress | | 10,000 |
| Cost of finished goods made | | 2,510,000 |
| | | 20,000 |
| | | 2,490,000 |

*Example 25b*
### Forecast trading and profit and loss account of 'Makes Co.' for the year ending 30 June

| | £ | £ |
|---|---|---|
| Sales | | |
| *Less* Cost of goods sold: | | 7,600,000 |
| Opening inventory of finished goods | 40,000 | |
| *Add* cost of goods manufactured | 2,490,000 | |
| | 2,530,000 | |
| *Deduct* closing inventory of finished goods | 30,000 | |
| | | |
| Gross profit | | 2,500,000 |
| *Less* Expenses: | | 5,100,000 |
| Wages and salaries | | |
| Selling and distribution | 3,750,000 | |

Forecast trading and profit and loss account of 'Makes Co.' – continued

|  | £ | £ |
|---|---|---|
| Heating and lighting | 250,000 | |
| Depreciation | 40,000 | |
| Financing charges | 120,000 | |
| Miscellaneous | 65,000 | |
| | 15,000 | |
| Net profit before tax | | 4,240,000 |
| | | £860,000 |

*Example 25c*

Forecast balance sheet of 'Makes Co.' as at 30 June

|  | £ | £ |  | £ | £ |
|---|---|---|---|---|---|
| Land and buildings | 5,400,000 | | Capital | | 2,810,000 |
| *Less* depreciation | 2,300,000 | | Reserves | | 2,320,000 |
| | | 3,100,000 | Loans | | 500,000 |
| Plant and machinery | 1,960,000 | | | | |
| *Less* depreciation | 660,000 | | | | |
| | | 1,300,000 | | | |
| Motor vehicles | 320,000 | | | | |
| *Less* depreciation | 60,000 | | | | |
| | | 260,000 | | | |
| Current assets: | | | Current liabilities: | | |
| Inventory of raw materials | 60,000 | | Creditors | 70,000 | |
| Inventory of work in progress | 20,000 | | Accruals | 20,000 | |
| Inventory of finished goods | 30,000 | | | | 90,000 |
| | 110,000 | | | | |
| Debtors | 940,000 | | | | |
| Bank | 10,000 | | | | |
| | | 1,060,000 | | | |
| | | 5,720,000 | | | 5,720,000 |

*Example 25d*

## Budget relationships

| | |
|---|---|
| Opening inventory of raw materials <br> Raw materials purchased <br> Closing inventory of raw materials | Materials budget |
| Direct manufacturing wages | Labour budget |
| Direct expenses | Expenses budget |
| Salaries and wages | Labour budget |
| Materials <br> Heating and lighting <br> Rent and rates | Expenses budget |
| Depreciation | Capital assets budget |
| Work in progress <br>   Opening <br>   Closing | Materials budget |
| Sales | Activity budget |
| Opening inventory of finished goods <br> Closing inventory of finished goods | Finished goods budget |
| Salaries and wages | Administration budget |
| Selling and distribution <br> Heating and lighting | Expenses budget |
| Financing changes | Financial budget |
| Miscellaneous | Expenses budget |
| Land and buildings <br> Plant and machinery <br> Motor vehicles <br> Depreciation | Capital asset budget |
| Inventory of raw materials <br> Inventory of work in progress | Materials budget |
| Inventory of finished goods | Finished goods budget |
| Debtors | Activity budget |
| Bank | Cash budget |
| Capital | Master budget |
| Resources | Master budget |
| Loans | Financial budget |
| Creditors | Materials budget |
| Accruals | Expenses budget |

## Managing Financial Information

*Example 26a*

The Council Tax to be levied for all bands in 2003/04 will be as follows:

| Estimated Valuation at 1 April 1991 | Band | Portsmouth City Council £ | Hampshire Police Authority £ | TOTAL £ | 2002/03 £ |
|---|---|---|---|---|---|
| Up to £40,000 | A | 599.40 | 64.86 | 664.26 | 550.20 |
| £40,001–£52,000 | B | 699.30 | 75.67 | 774.97 | 641.90 |
| £52,001–£68,000 | C | 799.20 | 86.48 | 885.68 | 733.60 |
| £68,001–£88,000 | D | 899.10 | 97.29 | 996.39 | 825.30 |
| £88,001–£120,000 | E | 1,098.90 | 118.91 | 1,217.81 | 1,008.70 |
| £120,001–£160,000 | F | 1,298.70 | 140.53 | 1,439.23 | 1,192.10 |
| £160,001–£320,000 | G | 1,498.50 | 162.15 | 1,660.65 | 1,375.50 |
| £320,000 and over | H | 1,798.20 | 194.58 | 1,992.78 | 1,650.60 |
| Southsea Town Council Precept | | | | 112,689 | 112,752 |
| Council Tax Base for Southsea Town Council | | | | 6,448.5 | 6,402.0 |
| Council Tax - Southsea Parish Purposes at Band D | | | | £17.48 | £17.61 |

*Example 26b*
**Calculation of the Council Tax 2003/04**

| **Portsmouth City Council** | *2003/04* £ | *2002/03* £ |
|---|---|---|
| Gross Expenditure | 420,138,301 | 385,878,966 |
| LESS Gross Income | 218,439,983 | 202,305,303 |
| Net Expenditure 2003/04 | 201,698,318 | 183,573,663 |
| LESS Revenue Support Grant/NDR Pool contribution | 149,909,318 | 139,910,483 |
| | 51,789,000 | 43,663,180 |
| ADD/(DEDUCT) Collection Fund Deficit (Surplus) at 31 March | (49,000) | (532,000) |
| Net Budget Requirement – Portsmouth City Council Purposes | 51,740,000 | 43,131,180 |
| Council Tax Base | 57,546.4 | 57,498.8 |
| Council Tax – Portsmouth City Council Purposes at Band D | | |
| $\dfrac{51,740,000}{57,546.4} =$ | £899.10 | £750.15 |
| Hampshire Police Authority Precept | 5,598,700 | 4,320,885 |
| Council Tax – Hampshire Police Authority Purposes at Band D | £97.29 | £75.15 |

**General balances**

| | £'000 |
|---|---|
| Balances 1 April 2002 | 4,521 |
| Reserves utilised 2002/03 | (146) |
| Estimated balances 1 April 2003 | 4,375 |
| Reserves utilised 2003/04 | (1,375) |
| Estimated balances 31 March 2004 | 3,000 |

*Example 26c*

**Revenue budget**  **Housing, health and social care portfolio (housing revenue account)**

| Actual 2001–2002 | Base Estimate 2002–03 | Revised Estimate 2002–03 | | Base Estimate 2003–04 |
|---|---|---|---|---|
| £ | £ | £ | **OTHER EXPENDITURE** | £ |
| 13,580,100 | 13,973,100 | 13,993,100 | Repairs and maintenance | 14,000,000 |
| 36,400 | 47,800 | 46,400 | Rent, Rates, Taxes and Other Charges | 47,800 |
| 25,525,400 | 25,889,800 | 26,414,500 | Rent rebates | 27,093,000 |
| 1,006,200 | 979,200 | 412,000 | Bad Debt provisions | 464,000 |
| 4,820,200 | 23,834,400 | 25,889,500 | Cost of capital charges | 26,777,400 |
| 19,229,800 | | | Capital expenditure charged to revenue | |
| | | | **Depreciation of fixed assets** | – |
| | | 11,108,200 | – Dwellings | 11,108,200 |
| | | 856,400 | – Other Assets | 868,400 |
| | | 32,000 | Debt management costs | 32,000 |
| | 300,000 | 31,200 | Contingency provision | 100,000 |
| **64,198,100** | **65,024,300** | **78,783,300** | | **80,490,800** |
| **76,526,100** | **78,775,900** | **92,988,600** | **Total Expenditure** | **95,821,800** |
| | | | **INCOME** | |
| | | | **Rents** | |
| 44,596,100 | 44,257,000 | 44,402,300 | Dwellings | 44,621,600 |
| 721,200 | 675,800 | 665,300 | Garages and Parking sites | 642,100 |
| 508,100 | 439,600 | 448,900 | Shops | 458,300 |
| 8,300 | 59,600 | 52,400 | Land Rents | 53,500 |
| 303,200 | 340,100 | 340,100 | **Fees and Charges** | – |
| 1,251,300 | 1,291,900 | 1,251,000 | General Charge | 570,000 |
| – | – | – | Heating Charges | 297,000 |
| 78,900 | 83,600 | 90,700 | Sheltered Housing Service Charge | 432,000 |
| | | | Supporting People Charge | 1,024,300 |
| (3,000) | 1,000 | 7,000 | Collection of Council Tax Income | 92,600 |
| 417,000 | 460,200 | 529,000 | Northern Electric commission | – |
| 888,500 | 1,010,700 | 1,096,400 | Liquidated Damages | 1,000 |
| 464,500 | 172,100 | 124,000 | Admin of Disposed Dwellings | 545,000 |
| | | | Leaseholders charges for Service & Facilities | 1,167,800 |
| 39,300 | 24,000 | | Other Charges for Services and Facilities | 126,800 |
| 237,000 | 604,000 | | | |
| | | | **Interest** | |
| – | 5,000 | – | Mortgage interest from sold homes | |
| 25,572,700 | 27,580,300 | 27,084,700 | Interest on balances | |
| – | – | – | | |
| 162,600 | 860,800 | 200,000 | **Government Grants** | – |
| 172,000 | 178,400 | 142,000 | Government Grants | – |
| 141,600 | – | 150,000 | HRA Subsidy Receivable | 27,633,400 |
| 75,559,300 | 78,044,100 | 76,583,800 | | – |
| | | | **Recovery of overpaid housing benefit** | 100,000 |
| | | | | – |
| | | | **Recharges to Other Services** | – |
| | | | Contribution from General Fund | 145,000 |
| | | | Contribution from General Fund | 150,000 |
| | | | | – |
| | | | Total Income | 78,060,400 |

*Example 26d*

## General Fund Summary: Appendix B

| Original Forecast Estimate 2002/03 £ | Revised Forecast Estimate 2002/03 £ | NET REQUIREMENTS OF PORTFOLIOS | Estimate 2003/04 £ | Forecast 2004/05 £ | Forecast 2005/06 £ |
|---|---|---|---|---|---|
| 14,346,500 | 14,384,800 | Culture and Leisure | 15,047,900 | 15,754,400 | 16,169,200 |
| 92,928,800 | 92,952,000 | Education and Lifelong Learning | 99,140,000 | 101,914,400 | 107,599,184 |
| 13,178,900 | 13,494,200 | Housing and Community | 13,677,500 | 14,035,400 | 14,392,600 |
| (743,500) | 580,000 | Leader | 1,446,700 | 2,245,700 | 2,201,000 |
| 3,554,700 | 3,833,700 | Planning Regeneration and Economic Development | 3,680,700 | 3,837,800 | 3,997,900 |
| 21,911,300 | 21,342,200 | Public Protection | 24,020,400 | 24,994,500 | 25,925,500 |
| 7,520,700 | 7,181,100 | Resources | 5,215,100 | 5,093,800 | 6,236,000 |
| 44,381,400 | 44,064,800 | Social & Health Care | 49,438,200 | 52,195,600 | 57,248,273 |
| 8,209,700 | 8,268,700 | Traffic & Transportation | 8,575,100 | 8,858,700 | 9,072,600 |
| 179,400 | 179,400 | General Purposes Committee | 191,300 | 203,400 | 216,000 |
| (16,900) | (16,900) | Licensing Committee | (13,000) | (9,000) | (4,900) |
| 27,700 | 27,700 | Development Control Committee | 28,600 | 29,500 | 30,400 |
| 940,000 | 940,000 | Public Service Agreement Grant Expenditure | 0 | 0 | 0 |
| **206,418,700** | **207,231,700** | **Portfolio Expenditure** | **220,448,500** | **229,154,200** | **243,083,757** |
| | | Other Expenditure | | | |
| 95,500 | 95,500 | Precepts | 97,900 | 100,300 | 102,800 |
| (102,500) | (102,500) | Portchester Crematorium – Share of Dividend | (105,000) | (107,500) | (110,000) |
| 160,000 | 160,000 | Compensatory Added Years Payments | 160,000 | 160,000 | 160,000 |
| 1,325,000 | 700,000 | Contingency Provision | 1,500,000 | 1,500,000 | 1,500,000 |
| 200,000 | 638,100 | Revenue Contributions to Capital Reserve | 1,000,000 | 1,000,000 | 1,000,000 |
| (21,910,200) | (23,003,700) | Asset Management Revenue Account | (20,260,400) | (19,854,900) | (19,391,800) |
| (940,000) | (940,000) | Public Service Agreement Grant Income | 0 | 0 | 0 |
| 52,400 | 90,800 | Other Expenditure | 232,400 | 275,000 | 318,700 |
| 0 | 0 | Top Slice | 0 | 0 | 0 |
| **(21,119,800)** | **(22,361,800)** | **Other Expenditure** | **(17,376,100)** | **(16,927,100)** | **(16,420,300)** |
| **185,298,900** | **184,869,900** | **TOTAL NET EXPENDITURE** | **203,073,400** | **212,227,100** | **226,663,457** |

## General Fund Summary: Appendix B – continued

| Original Forecast Estimate 2002/03 £ | Revised Forecast Estimate 2002/03 £ | | Estimate 2003/04 £ | Forecast 2004/05 £ | Forecast 2005/06 £ |
|---|---|---|---|---|---|
| | | NET REQUIREMENTS OF PORTFOLIOS | | | |
| | | FINANCED BY: | | | |
| 575,237 | 146,237 | Contribution from Balances and Reserves | 1,375,082 | (10,900) | 72,453 |
| 1,150,000 | 1,150,000 | Contribution from POC Reserve | 0 | 0 | 0 |
| 81,744,009 | 81,744,009 | Revenue Support Grant | 93,301,791 | | ( |
| 58,166,474 | 58,166,474 | Business Rate Income | 56,607,527 | 155,096,000 | 165,963.342 |
| 43,663,180 | 43,663,180 | Collection Fund (Tax at 19.9%) | 51,789,000 | 57,142,000 | 60,627,662 |
| 185,298,900 | 184,869,900 | | 203,073,400 | 212,227,100 | 226,663,457 |
| | | GENERAL FUND BALANCES | | | |
| 3,575,193 | 4,521,372 | Balance brought forward at 1 April | 4,375,135 | 3,000,053 | 3,010,953 |
| (575,237) | (146,237) | Add Surplus / Deduct (Deficit) for Year | (1,375,082) | 10,900 | (72.453) |
| 2,999,956 | 4,375,135 | **Balance carried forward at 31 March** | 3,000,053 | 3,010,953 | 2,938,500 |
| 0 | 0 | **Deficit to be Funded** | 0 | 0 | 61,600 |

145

# THE CASH BUDGET

At the end of this section the reader should understand the cash budget and the way in which the human resources manager would use it to control the cash resources of the department. Critically, as we saw in the previous chapter, the cash budget is used to plan and control the cash balances on a day-to-day basis. Money, like the other resources employed in organisations, is costly and should not be allowed to sit around doing nothing. It should be continuously working, and to have too much is as bad as having too little. The working capital is derived by taking the current liabilities away from the current assets of the undertaking, and is used to pay the running costs until more money is earned. The overall measure of the concern's liquidity and of its ability to pay its way is the amount of money it has readily available, which is generally represented by the cash in hand and cash at bank.

In drawing up the cash budget the only figure that is known with absolute certainty is the opening balance, which is the amount of money that is in hand or overdrawn at the start of the budget period. The rest of the items are largely estimates, or informed guesses, based on past experience and taking into account present and expected conditions. The receipts from the sale of goods, or the number of hours' service provided, or rent for accommodation, will rarely be what is due or has been earned, but will rather be what has been earned minus late receipts of cash. For example, in a particular month a local authority may have charged rates of £70,000 but the payments received might be only £50,000. This sort of difference between what should be received and what is actually received should be catered for in the cash budget.

The same technique should be applied item by item, and those responsible for drawing up the budget should always remember that things will rarely happen exactly as expected. The government, with some of the best brains in the world at its disposal, was unable to get its forecast right when it launched the BP flotation and its annual budget is never 100 per cent correct so ordinary mortals should not be too despondent when their plans go awry. Constant monitoring keeps any problems to a minimum.

Payments by organisations to their suppliers are just as likely to be delayed as receipts from customers, and it should be remembered that, within reasonable limits, account departments control when they make payments, whereas they do not have nearly so much say over when monies are received. Purchases may be paid for anything up to three months after the goods have been received, and some concerns wait even longer than that. The danger is that suppliers will become so tired of waiting for their money that any further goods are supplied on a cash-only basis or, what is perhaps worse, rumours will circulate that the organisation is having cash-flow problems and people refuse to deal with it at all. An extreme example of delayed payment would be: purchases for one month £20,000, payments for purchases £0. This, however, will generally occur only in the very early months of an undertaking, or when it is undergoing some sort of restructuring or other problem. More usually the figures would be something like: purchases £20,000, payments £12,000.

The illustration of a cash budget in Example 27 is not meant to be comprehensive but it does include many of the more usually encountered items. Once you have studied it, use a similar structure to solve Exercises 25, 26, and 27.

The budget shows a cash deficit of £12,000 at the end of December, but it should not cause too great a problem: if the cash budget has been closely monitored the accountant will be aware of it in plenty of time to arrange an overdraft facility with the bank or other financing. If this proves impossible it may be feasible to delay some of the capital expenditure, or if none of these solutions is possible the company could be sold as a going concern before things got out of hand. Each month the actual position

*Example 27a*

Cash budget for three months to 31 December

| | October | | November | | December | |
|---|---|---|---|---|---|---|
| | *Plan* | *Actual* | *Plan* | *Actual* | *Plan* | *Actual* |
| | £ | | £ | | £ | |
| Opening balance in hand (overdrawn) | (4,000) | | 59,000 | | 27,000 | |
| Receipts from sales: | | | | | | |
| this month | 80,000 | | 90,000 | | 88,000 | |
| previous month | 104,000 | | 120,000 | | 130,000 | |
| Total | 180,000 | | 269,000 | | 245,000 | |
| *Less* Payments for goods | | | | | | |
| this month | – | | 45,000 | | 60,000 | |
| previous month | 40,000 | | 60,000 | | 70,000 | |
| Wages and salaries | 50,000 | | 20,000 | | 20,000 | |
| Heating and lighting | 20,000 | | – | | 4,000 | |
| Transport | – | | 10,000 | | 15,000 | |
| Rates | 5,000 | | – | | 10,000 | |
| Capital items: | | | | | | |
| Purchase of fixed assets | – | | 100,000 | | 50,000 | |
| Postage and stationery | – | | 1,000 | | 2,000 | |
| Telephones | 2,000 | | 4,000 | | 5,000 | |
| Loan interest | 3,000 | | – | | 20,000 | |
| Miscellaneous | 1,000 | | 2,000 | | 1,000 | |
| Total | 121,000 | | 242,000 | | 257,000 | |
| Balance c/f in hand (overdrawn) | 59,000 | | 27,000 | | (£12,000) | |

is compared with the plan; to be useful the information must be available within at least a week of the month end and if possible sooner than that. Many undertakings monitor their cash on a daily basis and employ a computerised information system to enable them to do so, with any surplus monies being invested on the overnight market.

Let us now apply the techniques of the cash budget to the role of the human resources manager. The human resources department is generally treated as a cost centre that provides little financial benefit to the organisation. We have seen that this view can be challenged by an efficient human resources manager not only on the grounds of monies generated by selling training and recruitment facilities to outside organisations but also by demonstrating the savings that accrue when properly recruited and trained staff are working effectively. Indeed it might be argued that the human resources department is a profit centre rather than a cost centre.

The cash budget for a human resources department will employ exactly the same principles as those already described but the headings might be slightly different. Such a cash budget might look like Examples 27a and b.

*Example 27b*

|  | January | | February | | March | |
|---|---|---|---|---|---|---|
|  | Plan | Actual | Plan | Actual | Plan | Actual |
| Opening balance | | | | | | |
| RECEIPTS | | | | | | |
| Training | | | | | | |
| Recruitment | | | | | | |
|  | | | | | | |
| PAYMENTS | | | | | | |
| Employees | | | | | | |
| Training | | | | | | |
| Recruitment | | | | | | |
| Travelling | | | | | | |
| Materials | | | | | | |
| Business rate | | | | | | |
| Electricity | | | | | | |
| Postage | | | | | | |
| Telephone | | | | | | |
| Services | | | | | | |
| Capital | | | | | | |
| Miscellaneous | | | | | | |
| TOTAL | | | | | | |
| Balance c/f | | | | | | |

By comparing the planned with the actual activity on a monthly basis, the human resources manager can ensure that effective corrective action is taken. Estimates of payments are generally speaking easier to make accurately than estimates of income, although with practice both will improve.

This chapter illustrates the preparation of the master budget and its links with the subsidiary budgets that provide the information employed in its preparation. It also emphasises the importance of the cash budget and the need to monitor it on a regular and frequent basis.

Attempt the following exercises and compare your answers with those suggested at the back of the book.

## Exercise 25

Peter Brown intends to make and sell wooden models of famous sports personalities. Each model takes eight hours to make. Brown charges £8 per hour for his labour and uses mahogany costing £30; he adds 50 per cent to the cost price to arrive at his selling price and feels that there is a market for his product. Research has made him believe that, once he is established and his product becomes known, he will be able to sell 10 models a week, and he would like to maintain a buffer stock of three of the most popular models. He gives four weeks' credit and anticipates the demand to be: week 1–3 no sales; weeks 4 and 5, six sales; weeks 6 onward, 10 sales. His other costs will be rent of a shed, £10 per week; postage and stationery, £231 per week; rates, electricity and telephone, £1,200 per quarter, paid in March, June, September and December. The wood is purchased and paid for monthly in advance, with enough for 40 models, and stored on racks in the shed. Brown has brought in £10,000 as capital, and he has bought equipment for £8,000, leaving a cash balance of £2,000. The business is to start on 1 January. Draw up the cash budget for the six months January to June, assuming that Brown withdraws £200 per week for living expenses and pays for additional equipment costing £5,000 in June. Would you recommend Brown to start the business?

## Exercise 26

Draw up the cash budget from the following information for the six months from 1 July to 31 December.

- Opening cash balance at 1 July £3,000.
- Sales at £40 per unit:

|  | April | May | June | July | Aug | Sept | Oct | Nov | Dec |
|---|---|---|---|---|---|---|---|---|---|
| Units | 220 | 240 | 280 | 320 | 360 | 380 | 260 | 160 | 140 |

Debtors will pay two months after they have bought the goods.
- Payment for goods two months after they have been sold.

- £10 per unit direct labour payable in the same month as production.
- Raw materials cost £12 per unit, paid for three months after the goods are used in production.
- Production in units:

|  | April | May | June | July | Aug | Sept | Oct | Nov | Dec | Jan |
|---|---|---|---|---|---|---|---|---|---|---|
| Units | 300 | 340 | 360 | 400 | 260 | 220 | 200 | 180 | 140 | 120 |

- Other variable expenses are £6 per unit. Two-thirds of this cost is paid for in the same month as production and one-third in the month following production.
- Fixed expenses of £300 per month are paid one month in arrears.
- Capital expenditure for September £20,000.

## Exercise 27

The balance sheet for Dave's Delicatessen is shown below. Prepare a cash budget showing Dave's bank balance or overdraft for each month in the half year ending 30 April.

- Sales are budgeted to be:

| November | December | January | February | March | April |
|---|---|---|---|---|---|
| £6,000 | £10,000 | £7,000 | £23,000 | £4,000 | £8,000 |

- Some sales are on credit and the proportions are on average: credit 10 per cent, cash 90 per cent. Credit customers pay in the month following the sales.
- The gross profit margin is 25 per cent of selling price.
- Stocks are maintained at a constant level throughout the year.
- Half the purchases are paid for in the same month as they are purchased and 50 per cent in the subsequent month.
- Wages and other running expenses are £2,000 per month, paid in the month in which they are incurred.
- Premises and fittings are depreciated at 10 per cent per annum on cost.

The balance sheet of Dave's Delicatessen at 31 October

| | £ | £ | | £ |
|---|---|---|---|---|
| Premises | 10,000 | | Capital | 13,750 |
| Depreciation | 2,000 | | Creditors | 3,000 |
| | | 8,000 | Overdraft | 1,050 |
| Fittings | 8,000 | | | |
| Depreciation | 4,000 | 4,000 | | |
| Stock | | 5,000 | | |
| Debtors | | 800 | | |
| | | 17,800 | | 17,800 |

## SELF-TEST QUESTIONS (CASH BUDGET)

1. Why is the cash budget important?
2. What is liquidity measured by?
3. Why should corrective action be taken quickly when actual figures differ from the budget?
4. Why is it usually easier to estimate expenditure than to estimate cash receipts?

## Work-based assignment

Prepare a cash budget for your department. Discuss the figures that you arrive at with the human resources manager and/or the accountant.

## SELF-TEST QUESTIONS (MASTER BUDGET)

5. What are the constituent parts of the master budget?
6. How does the master budget link with the other budgets of an undertaking?
7. How may the human resources manager influence the master budget?
8. What will happen if the master budget reveals a situation that is disliked by the planning team?

## Work-based assignment

Discuss the master budget of your organisation with the accountant and ascertain the process by which it is prepared.

# Capital Budgeting and its Application to Human Resources

## OBJECTIVE

At the end of this chapter you will understand the process of capital budgeting and be able to employ the pay-back, accounting rate of return and discounted cash flow techniques to justify proposed capital expenditure. The management standards that will be developed by this chapter are 'critically appraising proposals for capital projects' and 'evaluating the financial implications of sustainable development'.

All systems of budgetary control are important and require the utmost care in their preparation and monitoring, but whilst revenue budgets commit an organisation for only a short period of time, normally one year, capital schemes can commit them to expenditure for 10 or more years. The capital budget of an undertaking in its original draft may be drawn up on similar lines to Example 28 below for the next 10 years.

*Example 28*

Capital budget

| Project | Total £(000) | Year 1 £(000) | Year 2 £(000) | Year 3 £(000) | Year 4 £(000) | Year 5 £(000) | Year 6 £(000) | Year 7 £(000) | Year 8 £(000) | Year 9 £(000) | Year 10 £(000) |
|---|---|---|---|---|---|---|---|---|---|---|---|
| A | 22,300 | 4,000 | 8,000 | 10,000 | 300 | | | | | | |
| B | 22,290 | | | 400 | 900 | 7,500 | 12,800 | 690 | | | |
| C | 650 | 600 | 50 | | | | | | | | |
| D | 16,000 | 12,500 | 2,500 | 1,000 | | | | | | | |
| E | 33,200 | 7,000 | 200 | 9,000 | 8,000 | 6,000 | 2,400 | 600 | | | |
| F | 24,000 | | | | | | | | | | |
| G | 43,800 | | | 7,000 | 15,000 | 20,000 | 1,200 | 500 | | | |
| H | 33,700 | | 7,600 | 19,400 | 6,200 | 500 | | | | | |
| I | 8,000 | | | | 8,000 | | | | 4,000 | 8,000 | 12,000 |
| J | 140 | 40 | | | | | | | 100 | | |
| K | 10 | 10 | | | | | | | | | |
| L | 60 | 60 | | | | | | | | | |
| M | 15 | | 15 | | | | | | | | |
| TOTAL | 204,065 | 24,210 | 18,365 | 46,800 | 38,400 | 34,000 | 16,400 | 1,790 | 4,100 | 8,000 | 12,000 |

The budget committee would focus most strongly on years 1 and 2, but as concerns face more demands on their resources than the resources available, some method of deciding which among competing schemes should go forward for further consideration has to be devised. It is important to emphasise that the methods of helping to eliminate some schemes do not make the decision; all they do is give the decision-maker additional information on which to act.

There are four generally accepted methods of 'capital rationing' that are of help in deciding which schemes should be allowed to go forward for further consideration: pay-back, rate of return, discounted cash flow and cost–benefit analysis. Each of them is useful to the human resources manager when making bids for money to invest in capital schemes.

# PAY-BACK

This enables the time taken to recover the initial investment – either through additional money coming into the organisation or by reducing the cash outflow – to be calculated. The result can then be compared with the desired pay-back period, which might be three years. Schemes that meet the criterion – ie. that they have a pay-back of three years or less – go forward for consideration, whilst the others are excluded. Example 29 shows such a system of pay-back.

## Example 29

The human resources department requires a piece of machinery that costs £30,000 and is more efficient than the existing machine, resulting in an annual saving in operating cost, excluding depreciation, over five years of: £6,000 in year 1, £8,000 in year 2 and £10,000 in years 3–5. The pay-back in this case, provided the savings are generated equally throughout the year, would be:

*Example 29*

|  | £ | £ | £ |
|---|---|---|---|
| Cost |  | *Cumulative* | 30,000 |
| *Pay-back* |  |  |  |
| Year 1 | 6,000 | 6,000 |  |
| Year 2 | 8,000 | 14,000 |  |
| Year 3 | 10,000 | 24,000 |  |
| Year 4 (7.2 months) | 6,000 | 30,000 |  |

In this case pay-back takes three years and 7.2 months, so that if the three years' pay-back was the sole criterion the scheme would not go forward for further consideration.

Budget holders are concerned with the speed at which their outlay is recovered, so this method of capital rationing is frequently met in practice. It is easy to understand and apply, but it has the disadvantage of ignoring what happens once pay-back has been achieved and does not review the scheme as a whole. On the other hand, it has the advantage of recognising, even if only indirectly, that money recovered earlier is more valuable than money received later, because money that you have can be invested and earn interest, and because of this gives some recognition of the "time value" of money.

## ACCOUNTING RATE OF RETURN

The accounting rate of return is calculated by expressing the average annual cash flow generated by the scheme as a percentage of the outlay.

Applying the cash flow shown in Example 28, we have:

Outlay £30,000

Average annual cash flows:

$$\frac{£6,000 + £8,000 + £10,000 + £10,000 + £10,000}{5 \text{ years}} = \frac{£44,000}{5}$$

$$= £8,800 \text{ p.a.}$$

The average annual cash flow of £8,800 is then expressed as a percentage of the outlay of £30,000:

$$= \frac{£8,800 \times 100}{£30,000} = 29.3\%$$

If the organisation was looking for a return of 30 per cent this scheme would be excluded, but if 25 per cent was the required rate it would go forward for further consideration. This method is not as commonly employed as the pay-back, although it is relatively easy to understand and apply and it does review the whole scheme. Its disadvantage is that it ignores the time value of money: that is, £1 received today is treated as having the same value as £1 received in 10 years' time, which is nonsense in view of the opportunities for investing the money available now.

## DISCOUNTED CASH FLOW (NET PRESENT VALUE)

This approach is considered to be superior to both pay-back and accounting rate of return because it considers both the true value of money and the whole life of the scheme. The basis of the approach is that if you have £1 (sterling) today you can invest it and earn interest at say 5 per cent. If on the other hand you have to wait a year before you receive £1, you have lost the opportunity to earn a year's interest. In view of this, £1 that you have today is more valuable than £1 that you are going to receive at some time in the future. Discount tables can be used to reflect this difference in value. Those for 8 per cent, 15 per cent and 16 per cent discount rates are shown in the Appendix, but tables are available for all the discount rates that are likely to be required.

Applying discounted cash flow techniques to arrive at the net present value of the scheme, and assuming that the organisation requires a 16 per cent return on investment, we have:

## Example 30

| | | | |
|---|---|---|---|
| Outlay | | | £30,000 |
| Savings: | Discount factor | | |
| Year 1 | £ 6,000 × 0.8621 | = | 5172.6 |
| Year 2 | £ 8,000 × 0.7432 | = | 5945.6 |
| Year 3 | £10,000 × 0.6407 | = | 6407 |
| Year 4 | £10,000 × 0.5523 | = | 5523 |
| Year 5 | £10,000 × 0.4761 | = | 4761 |
| Present value of the future cash flows | | | £27,809.2 |
| Net present value of scheme | | | −£2,190.8 |

In this calculation the discount figure of 0.8621 in year 1, and those for the other years, are obtained from discount tables like those in the Appendix. The relevant table is the 16 per cent table, and the column used is 'Present value of £1'. This process can be considerably speeded up when the same sum of money is involved in each year, because it is then possible to use the 'Present value of £1 received at the end of period' column just once, as has been done in Solutions 28, 29 and 31.

The present value of the future cash flows is less than the outlay of £30,000, which means that the scheme is not making the required 16 per cent on the investment and should not go forward for further consideration. This approach to capital rationing is frequently employed because it reviews the whole scheme and recognises the time value of money. Tables are prepared showing the appropriate rate by which to multiply at various time intervals and costs of money.

There is a growing tendency for organisations to use a combination of pay-back and net present value in capital rationing when preparing their capital budgets, but it should be borne in mind that, although capital budgeting is essential, a great deal of capital expenditure takes place on the basis of pure necessity rather than because it has been planned for. Machinery breaks down or has to be replaced by new technology, so it should always be remembered that the budget is a plan and not a straitjacket. Different people need different things to help them in their planning, decision-making and control, and it is essential that the management information system gives the right information to the right people and at the right time. The human resources manager needs to keep in mind the criteria that have to be met before schemes requiring capital expenditure are agreed, otherwise all proposals for capital expenditure in the department may be rejected. The effective manager will ensure the department proposals for capital expenditure meet the required pay-back, rate of return or discounted cash flow requirements. It is no use to propose outlay on new equipment that will produce more effective training if the pay-back is five years whilst the organisation requires three years. Neither would a return of 8 per cent be considered if the organisation expects 10 per cent. To keep submitting schemes that fail to meet the hurdle rates simply ruins the credibility of the department and is in no one's interest because the undertaking as a whole suffers from the inefficiencies of a major constituent.

## COST–BENEFIT ANALYSIS

Cost–benefit analysis is based on the concept of social costs and benefits. For example, a factory may pollute the atmosphere with the waste material from the manufacturing process, which would be a social cost. Its owner may then build a beautiful house that improves the view for the general population, which is a social benefit. The difficulty lies in valuing the cost and benefit to see which is greater. Cost–benefit analysis methods are advocated for dealing with capital projects in which investments are large and indivisible, group wants are catered for and economic prices are not charged to consumers for use of the final output. Viewed as a purely commercial proposition from the point of view of London Transport, the Jubilee Line is not attractive, though if fares could be charged at an economic rate it could be a profitable investment. In attempting to calculate the costs and benefits of the Jubilee Line the general headings employed would have been:

*Example 31*

General headings for the Jubilee Line

| | | £m | Present value at X % discount |
|---|---|---|---|
| COSTS | Capital outlay | | |
| | Annual working costs | | |
| BENEFITS | Traffic diverted to Jubilee Line | | |
| | (1) Underground time, comfort | | |
| | (2) Railway's time | | |
| | (3) Buses' time | | |
| | (4) Motorists' time, cost | | |
| | (5) Pedestrians' time | | |

This would be the skeleton of the final appraisal and you can see the problems involved in putting a monetary value on many of the benefits as well as in arriving at an appropriate rate of discount. The fact that cost–benefit analysis is difficult to apply does not mean that it should be ignored. It is in fact used frequently where major public works are considered and is becoming more popular due to the perceived impact of global warming on all our lives.

*Sustainability* is an extension of cost–benefit analysis and is of growing concern to governments and organisations all over the world. The concept endeavours to enable undertakings to meet current needs whilst safeguarding the interest of future generations. The way in which this is achieved is by the wider application of cost–benefit analysis, as for example when the public became aware that some retailers were selling goods manufactured by child labour. Consumers ceased buying the goods and the retailers concerned had to revise their policy whilst their competitors took advantage of the situation. Organisations like Legal & General, Sony and the Scottish Agricultural College focus on sustainable development in their decision-making, and it is essential that the human resources manager bears this in mind when involved in this process. Sustainable development strategies not only bring social and environmental benefits but can also provide improved job satisfaction through greater commitment, as demonstrated by The Body Shop.

This chapter explains the four main methods of evaluating competing capital schemes or justifying capital expenditure: pay-back, accounting rate of return, discounted cash flow, and cost–benefit analysis. It also explores the financial implications of sustainable development and its increasing importance in the current world situation.

Work through Exercises 28, 29, 30 and 31 and compare your answers with those suggested at the back of the book.

## Exercise 28

Green is concerned about production costs and after extensive enquiries has identified a new machine that will carry out the required process much more effectively than the present one. The machine costs £80,000 and will last for eight years, during which time running costs and maintenance will be reduced by £10,000 a year and there will be a saving on materials of £4,000 a year. Would you recommend Green to buy the machine if the only consideration was a financial one and the cost of money was 15 per cent?

## Exercise 29

A local authority has decided that the heating costs of the human resources department are excessive and has received tenders for insulating the building. The costs of insulation are £130,000, inclusive of double-glazing and it is expected that the benefits will last for 15 years, after which the department will move to new premises. The estimated savings from the insulation are £16,000 a year and the cost of capital is 8 per cent. Should the insulation be undertaken on the basis of the financial information provided?

## Exercise 30

A human resources department is considering the purchase of a printing system for £8,000. The estimated cost savings from its use over the next five years are

| Year | £ |
|---|---|
| 1 | 1,000 |
| 2 | 2,000 |
| 3 | 4,000 |
| 4 | 2,000 |
| 5 | 1,000 |
| Total | 10,000 |

Should it be purchased if the department's cost of capital is 8 per cent?

## Exercise 31

Your organisation is considering expanding the human resouces department at a cost of £40,000. This will allow additional training to be provided over the next five years, increasing net income by £10,000 a year. If a return on investment of 8 per cent is required should the scheme be accepted?

## SELF-TEST QUESTIONS

1. What are the four methods of justifying capital expenditure?
2. What is the most common reason for capital expenditure?
3. How is the pay-back calculated?
4. How is the accounting rate of return calculated?
5. Which method of assessing capital schemes is most commonly employed?

## Work-based assignment

Ascertain the method(s) of ranking capital schemes employed in your organisation. What are they and how is the appropriate return arrived at?

# Solutions to Exercises

## SOLUTIONS TO CHAPTER 4
### Solution 1

Balance sheet of Sacha
as at 5 June

| Assets | | Liabilities | |
|---|---|---|---|
| Current assets: | | | |
| Bank | £60,000 | Capital | £60,000 |

### Solution 2

Balance sheet of Sacha
as at 6 June

| Assets | | Liabilities | |
|---|---|---|---|
| Fixed assets: | | Capital | £60,000 |
| Premises | £80,000 | Loan | £40,000 |
| Current assets: | | | |
| Bank | £20,000 | | |
| | £100,000 | | £100,000 |

It is assumed that the business borrowed the £40,000, and not Sacha. Had Sacha borrowed the money, then the capital would have become £100,000, with no loan appearing.

### Solution 3

Balance sheet of Sacha
as at 7 June

| Assets | | | Liabilities | |
|---|---|---|---|---|
| Fixed assets: | | | Capital | £61,500 |
| Premises | £80,000 | | Loan | £40,000 |
| Fixtures/fittings | £8,000 | | | |
| Motor vehicle | £1,500 | £89,500 | | |
| | | | | |
| Current assets: | | | | |
| Bank | | £12,000 | | |
| | | £101,500 | | £101,500 |

You can see that the capital has increased by £1,500. This is because the van that the owner has brought into the business becomes part of the capital, even though it has not been paid for. The bank balance is reduced by the £8,000 paid for the fixtures and fittings.

## Solution 4

Balance sheet of Sacha
as at 8 June

| Assets | | | Liabilities | |
|---|---|---|---|---|
| Fixed assets: | | | Capital | £61,500 |
| Premises | £80,000 | | Loan | £40,000 |
| Fixtures/fittings | £8,000 | | | |
| Motor vehicle | £1,500 | £89,500 | | |
| | | | | |
| Current assets: | | | Current liabilities: | |
| Inventory | £30,000 | | Creditors: | £20,000 |
| Bank | £2,000 | £32,000 | | |
| | | £121,500 | | £121,500 |

The creditors of £20,000 appear as a current liability, and the bank balance is reduced by the £10,000 paid, to £2,000. The inventory of £30,000 is a current asset.

## Solution 5

Balance sheet of Sacha
as at 9 June

| Assets | | | Liabilities | |
|---|---|---|---|---|
| Fixed assets: | | | Capital | £61,500 |
| Premises | £80,000 | | Reserves: | |
| Fixtures/fittings | £8,000 | | Retained profit | £40,000 |
| Motor vehicle | £1,500 | £89,500 | Loan | £40,000 |
| | | | | |
| Current assets: | | | Current liabilities: | |
| Inventory | £10,000 | | Creditors: | £20,000 |
| Debtors | £50,000 | | | |
| Bank | £12,000 | £72,000 | | |
| | | £161,500 | | £161,500 |

The retained profit of £40,000 under 'reserves' on the liabilities side is the profit made on the sale. On the assets side the changes take place in the current assets section, where inventory is reduced by £20,000 to £10,000, the bank balance is increased by £10,000 to £12,000, and debtors for the credit sales of £50,000 appear.

# Solution 6

### Balance sheet of Sacha
### as at 10 June

| Assets | | | Liabilities | |
|---|---|---|---|---|
| Fixed assets: | | | Authorized and issued | |
| Premises | £80,000 | | share capital: | |
| Fixtures/fittings | £8,000 | | 203,000 shares | |
| Motor vehicle | £1,500 | £89,500 | at 50p | £101,500 |
| | | | Loan | £40,000 |
| Current assets: | | | Current liabilities: | |
| Inventory | £10,000 | | Creditors: | £20,000 |
| Debtors | £50,000 | | | |
| Bank | £12,000 | £72,000 | | |
| | | £161,500 | | £161,500 |

The capital and reserves have been replaced by the authorised and issued share capital. The vertical form of the balance sheet would be:

### Balance sheet of Sacha
### as at 10 June

| | | |
|---|---|---|
| Fixed assets: | | |
| Premises | £80,000 | |
| Fixtures and fittings | £8,000 | |
| Motor vehicle | £1,500 | |
| | | £89,500 |
| Current assets: | | |
| Inventory | £10,000 | |
| Debtors | £50,000 | |
| Bank | £12,000 | |
| | £72,000 | |
| Less Current liabilities: | | |
| Creditors | £20,000 | |
| Working capital | | £52,000 |
| Net capital employed | | £141,500 |
| Less Loan | | £40,000 |
| | | £101,500 |
| Financed by | | |
| Authorised and issued share capital: | | |
| 203,000 shares at 50p each | | £101,500 |

We have worked together through a series of balance sheets and you have completed some exercises to give you a good understanding of the structure of the balance sheet and the items that would be of greatest interest to the HR manager. A more detailed interpretation of the information it contains (and its relevance to HR managers) will appear in Chapter 7 when the accounts of Marks & Spencer will be analysed.

# SOLUTIONS TO CHAPTER 5
## Solution 7

Trading and profit and loss account of Thomas for the first four weeks

|  | £ | £ | £ |
|---|---|---|---|
| Sales |  |  | 4,240 |
| Cost of goods sold: |  |  |  |
| Opening inventory |  | 0 |  |
| *Add* inventory purchased |  | 2,600 |  |
|  |  | 2,600 |  |
| *Less* closing inventory |  | 120 |  |
| Cost of goods sold |  |  | 2,480 |
| Gross profit |  |  | 1,760 |
| Less Expenses: |  |  |  |
| Rent of yard |  | 160 |  |
| Weekend help |  | 180 |  |
| Obstruction fines |  | 140 |  |
| Depreciation: |  |  |  |
| Stall | 20 |  |  |
| Scales | 7 | 27 | 507 |
| Net profit |  |  | 1,253 |

Cash statement

|  | £ | £ |
|---|---|---|
| Opening balance |  | 5,000 |
| *Add* money received from sales |  | 4,240 |
|  |  | 9,240 |
| *Less* payments: |  |  |
| Rent of yard | 120 |  |
| Help | 180 |  |
| Fines | 140 |  |
| Scales | 586 |  |
| Stall | 1,140 |  |
| Fruit | 2,600 |  |
|  |  | 4,766 |
| Closing cash in hand |  | 4,474 |

Balance sheet of Thomas
as at the end of the first four weeks

| | £ | £ | | £ |
|---|---|---|---|---|
| Fixed assets: | | | Capital | 5,000 |
| Scales | 586 | | Reserves: | |
| Less depreciation | 7 | 579 | Retained profit | 1,253 |
| Stall | 1,140 | | | |
| Less depreciation | 20 | 1,120 | | |
| | | 1,699 | | |
| Current assets: | | | | |
| Inventory | 120 | | Current liabilities: | |
| Cash | 4,474 | | Rent due | 40 |
| | | 4,594 | | ____ |
| | | 6,293 | | 6,293 |

Although a profit of £1,253 has been earned, the cash balance has fallen from £5,000 to £4,474. This means that the business has not generated enough funds for its needs, mainly owing to the purchase of the fixed assets. The depreciation was calculated as follows:

| | £ |
|---|---|
| Stall cost | 1,140 |
| *Less* scrap | 100 |
| | 1,040 |

divided by life, which is four years, giving 4 x 13 (which is the number of four-week periods in a year) = 52 periods. We then have:

$$\frac{1040}{52} = £20 \text{ per four week period}$$

| | £ |
|---|---|
| Scales cost | 586 |
| *Less* scrap | 40 |
| | 546 |

divided by life, which is six years, giving:

$$\frac{546}{(6 \times 13)} = \frac{546}{78} = £7 \text{ per four week period}$$

The closing stock is valued at the lowest of cost or current market value. The rent of £160 is the rent that should be paid. ie four weeks at £40 per week, whether or not this is actually paid.

# Solution 8

Trading and profit and loss account of Thomas for the second four weeks

| | £ | £ | £ |
|---|---|---|---|
| Sales | | | 5,000 |
| Cost of goods sold: | | | |
| Opening inventory | | 120 | |
| *Add* inventory purchased | | 3,900 | |
| | | 4,020 | |
| *Less* closing inventory | | 400 | |
| Cost of goods sold | | | 3,620 |
| Gross profit | | | 1,380 |
| Less Expenses: | | | |
| Rent | | 160 | |
| Fines | | 260 | |
| Help | | 180 | |
| Depreciation: | | | |
| Stall | 20 | | |
| Scales | 7 | | |
| | | 27 | |
| Insurance premium | | 16 | |
| | | | 643 |
| Net profit | | | 737 |

| Cash statement | | | |
|---|---|---|---|
| | £ | £ | £ |
| Opening balance | | | 4,474 |
| *Add* money received from sales | | | 5,000 |
| | | | 9,474 |
| *Less* Payments: | | | |
| Rent | | 120 | |
| Fines | | 260 | |
| Help | | 180 | |
| Household expenses | | 400 | |
| Fruit | | 3,900 | |
| Insurance | | 208 | |
| | | | 5,068 |
| Closing cash in hand | | | 4,406 |

The insurance of £16 is given by taking one thirteenth of the £208 paid.

Balance sheet of Thomas
as at the end of the second four weeks

| | £ | £ | | £ | £ |
|---|---|---|---|---|---|
| Fixed assets: | | | Capital | | 5000 |
| Scales | 586 | | Reserves: | | |
| Less depreciation | 14 | 572 | Retained profit | | |
| Stall | 1,140 | | First four weeks | 1,253 | |
| Less depreciation | 40 | 1,100 | Second four weeks | 737 | |
| | | 1,672 | | 1,990 | |
| Current assets: | | | Less household | | |
| Insurance, pre-paid | 192 | | money (drawings) | 400 | 1,590 |
| Inventory | 400 | | Current liabilities: | | |
| Cash | 4,406 | | Rent due | | 80 |
| | | 4,998 | | | |
| | | 6,670 | | | 6,670 |

A further profit of £737 has been made in the second four weeks but the cash balance has been reduced by £68, owing largely to the drawings and increased inventory. Generally it is bad to remove all the profit from a business, but £400 drawings seem reasonable out of a profit of £737, particularly as there is a large sum of money in the business.

## Solution 9

Trading and profit and loss account of Thomas for the third four weeks

| | £ | £ | £ |
|---|---|---|---|
| Sales | | | 6,000 |
| Cost of goods sold: | | | |
| Opening inventory | | 400 | |
| Add purchases of fruit | | 5,000 | |
| | | 5,400 | |
| Deduct closing inventory | | 600 | 4,800 |
| Gross profit | | | 1,200 |
| Less Expenses: | | | |
| Rent | | 160 | |
| Fines | | 300 | |
| Help | | 180 | |
| Depreciation: | | | |
| Stall | 20 | | |
| Scales | 7 | 27 | |
| Insurance | | 16 | 683 |
| Net operating profit | | | 517 |
| Loss on sale of stall | | | 280 |
| Net profit | | | 237 |

The operating profit is the profit from normal business operations and excludes unusual or extraordinary items like the profit or loss on the sale of fixed assets. The accounting convention of anticipating losses has been followed by making a provision for the expected fine.

Sale of stall

|  | £ |
|---|---|
| Original cost of stall | 1,140 |
| *Less* total depreciation ($20 \times 3$) | 60 |
| Book value of the stall | 1,080 |
| Proceeds of the sale | 800 |
| Loss on the sale | 280 |

Cash statement

|  | £ | £ |
|---|---|---|
| Opening balance | | 4,406 |
| *Add* sales receipts | | 6,000 |
| Receipt from sale of stall | | 800 |
| | | 11,206 |
| *Deduct* payments: | | |
| Delivery van | 5,100 | |
| Fruit | 5,000 | |
| Household expenses | 600 | |
| Rent | 200 | |
| Help | 180 | |
| | | 11,080 |
| Closing cash in hand | | 126 |

The balance sheet is shown on the next page

A further operating profit of £517 has seen the cash balance reduced to £126 because of the purchase of the delivery van. Thomas will have to go through a period of consolidation if he is to stabilise his cash situation.

## Balance sheet of Thomas
### as at the end of the third four weeks

| | £ | £ | £ | £ | £ |
|---|---|---|---|---|---|
| Fixed assets: | | | | | |
| Van | | | | | 5,000 |
| Scales | 586 | 5,100 | | | |
| Less depreciation | 21 | 565 | | | |
| | | 5,665 | | | |
| Capital | | | | | |
| Reserves: | | | | | |
| Retained profit | | | | | |
| First four weeks | | | | 1,253 | |
| Second four weeks | | | | 737 | |
| Third four weeks | | | | 237 | |
| | | | | 2,227 | |
| Less drawings | | | | | |
| Second four weeks | | | 400 | | |
| Third four weeks | | | 600 | 1,000 | |
| | | | | | 1,227 |
| Current liabilities: | | | | | |
| Rent due | | | | 40 | |
| Fine pending | | | | 300 | 340 |
| Current assets: | | | | | |
| Insurance prepaid | 176 | | | | |
| Inventory | 600 | | | | |
| Cash | 126 | 902 | | | |
| | | 6,567 | | | 6,567 |

# Solution 10

Trading and profit and loss account of Thomas for the fourth four weeks

|  | £ | £ | £ |
|---|---|---|---|
| Sales |  |  | 6,500 |
| Cost of goods sold: |  |  |  |
| Opening inventory |  | 600 |  |
| *Add* purchases of fruit and vegetables |  | 6,500 |  |
|  |  | 7,100 |  |
| *Deduct* closing inventory |  | 1,700 |  |
|  |  |  | 5,400 |
| Gross profit |  |  | 1,100 |
| *Add* overprovision for fine recovered |  |  | 160 |
|  |  |  | 1,260 |
| *Deduct* expenses: |  |  |  |
| Rent |  | 160 |  |
| Help |  | 180 |  |
| Vehicle running |  | 100 |  |
| Vehicle licence |  | 10 |  |
| Insurance |  | 16 |  |
| Depreciation |  |  |  |
| Vehicle | 110 |  |  |
| Scales | 7 | 117 |  |
|  |  |  | 583 |
| Net profit |  |  | 677 |

The vehicle licence of £10 is calculated by taking one thirteenth of £130.

## Cash statement

|  | £ | £ |
|---|---|---|
| Opening balance |  | 126 |
| *Add* sales receipts |  | 6,100 |
|  |  | 6,226 |
| *Deduct* payments: |  |  |
| Inventory purchased for cash | 3,500 |  |
| Payments to creditor for inventory | 1,800 |  |
| Vehicle running expenses paid | 100 |  |
| Vehicle licence purchased | 130 |  |
| Rent | 160 |  |
| Help | 180 |  |
| Household expenses | 650 |  |
| Fine | 140 |  |
|  |  | 6,660 |
| Cash overdrawn |  | (434) |

Thomas' profit is £677. The balance sheet (on the next page) shows his financial position at the end of the fourth four weeks, but only on the assumption that the business is going to continue. If he were to close the business and sell his assets a very different picture could emerge. For example, the vehicle might realise £3,000 instead of the £4,990 shown in the books, and the scales £40 instead of the book value of £558. There is a problem with liquidity and Thomas may temporarily have to reduce spending on the family.

**Balance sheet of Thomas**
**as at the end of the fourth four weeks**

| | £ | £ | £ | | £ | £ | £ |
|---|---|---|---|---|---|---|---|
| **Fixed assets:** | | | | **Capital** | | | 5,000 |
| | | | | Reserves: | | | |
| Vehicle | 5,100 | | | First four weeks | 1,253 | | |
| Less depreciation | 110 | 4,990 | | Second four weeks | 737 | | |
| | | | | Third four weeks | 237 | | |
| Scales | 586 | | | Fourth four weeks | 677 | 2,904 | |
| Less depreciation | 28 | 558 | | Less drawings | | | |
| | | 5,548 | | Second four weeks | 400 | | |
| | | | | Third four weeks | 600 | | |
| | | | | Fourth four weeks | 650 | 1,650 | |
| | | | | | | | 1,254 |
| **Current assets:** | | | | **Current liabilities:** | | | |
| Insurance pre-paid | 160 | | | Rent due | 40 | | |
| Inventory | 1,700 | | | Creditor | 1,200 | | |
| Licence | 120 | | | Bank overdraft | 434 | | 1,674 |
| Debtors | 400 | 2,380 | | | | | |
| | | 7,928 | | | | | 7,928 |

# SOLUTIONS TO CHAPTER 7
## Solution 11

Thomas' ratios

|  | Period 1 | Period 2 | Period 3 | Period 4 |
|---|---|---|---|---|
| **Net profit as a percentage of the net capital employed** | | | | |
| $\dfrac{\text{Net profit} \times 100}{\text{Net capital employed}}$ | $\dfrac{£1,253 \times 100}{£6,253} = 20\%$ | $\dfrac{£737 \times 100}{£6,590} = 11.2\%$ | $\dfrac{£237 \times 100}{£6,227} = 3.8\%\ £6,590$ | $\dfrac{£677 \times 100}{£6,254} = 10.8\%$ |
| **Gross profit as a percentage of the net capital employed** | | | | |
| $\dfrac{\text{Gross profit} \times 100}{\text{Net capital employed}}$ | $\dfrac{£1,760 \times 100}{£6,253} = 28\%$ | $\dfrac{£1,380 \times 100}{£6,590} = 20.9\%$ | $\dfrac{£1,200 \times 100}{£6,227} = 19.3\%$ | $\dfrac{£1,100 \times 100}{£6,254} = 17.6\%$ |
| **Mark-up** | | | | |
| $\dfrac{(\text{Selling price} - \text{Cost price}) \times 100}{\text{Cost price}}$ | $\dfrac{£1,760 \times 100}{£2,480} = 71\%$ | $\dfrac{£1,380 \times 100}{£3,620} = 38.1\%$ | $\dfrac{£1,200 \times 100}{£4,800} = 25\%$ | $\dfrac{£1,100 \times 100}{£5,400} = 20.4\%$ |

## Thomas' ratios

| | Period 1 | Period 2 | Period 3 | Period 4 |
|---|---|---|---|---|
| *Current ratio* | | | | |
| Current assets:current liabilities | | | | |
| | £4,594:£40 = 115:1 | £4,998:£80 = 62:1 | £902:£340 = 2.6:1 | £2,380:£1,674 = 1.4:1 |
| *Quick ratio (acid test)* | | | | |
| Quick assets:current liabilities | | | | |
| | £4,474:40 = 111.9:1 | £4,598:£80 = 57.4:1 | £302:£340 = 0.89:1 | £680:£1,674 = 0.4:1 |
| *Rate of inventory turnover* | | | | |
| Cost of inventory sold / Average inventory | $\frac{£2,480}{£120}$ = 20.7 times | $\frac{£3,620}{£260}$ = 13.9 times | $\frac{£4,800}{£500}$ = 9.6 times | $\frac{£5,400}{£1,150}$ = 4.7 times |

*Age of debtors*: Not meaningful in this example

*Age of creditors*: Not meaningful in this example

# Solution 12

| World Games plc | | | | |
| --- | --- | --- | --- | --- |
| Profitability ratios | | 2002 | 2003 | 2004 |
| Return on capital employed (%) | | 14.5 | 8.1 | 9.2 |
| Profit margin (%) | | 15.3 | 11.9 | 10.6 |
| Capital turnover | | | | |
| Stock | Months | 7.4 | 8.6 | 11.1 |
| Debtors | Months | 2.5 | 2.7 | 2.9 |
| Fixed capital | Months | 7.5 | 12.0 | 9.4 |
| | | | Under control | |
| Liquidity ratios | | | | |
| Current ratio | Times | 4.5 | 4.2 | 2.1 |
| Acid test ratio | Times | 1.7 | 1.5 | 0.72 |

## *Analysis*

The return on capital employed shows a large decline between 2002 and 2003, 14.5 percent down to 8.1 per cent, and then a slight recovery to 9.2 per cent in 2004.

The profit margin reflects a similar decline from 15.3 per cent to 10.6 per cent over the three years, although the decline is much greater between 2002 and 2003.

The prime costs are under control and the increase in the proportions is expected to support the increased sales.

The rates of capital turnover are slowing most noticeably in the case of stock.

The liquidity ratios are declining and the business is failing to generate sufficient funds for its needs. It gives every impression of being an organisation run by an enthusiast to meet his needs. He will take on any work that he sees to be a challenge, which maintains his interest and enthusiasm but is bad for business.

He should decide what his business is about and endeavour to achieve a better flow of work. This will increase the overall efficiency of the organisation.

The human resources manager would talk to Mr. Davies to see whether he would be prepared to curb his enthusiasm. If he was not prepared to do so the business would fail and staff should be counselled accordingly.

The calculations for 2002 have been made on the basis shown below:

Return on capital employed

$$\frac{76,660 \times 100}{530,544} = 14.5 \text{ per cent}$$

Profit margin (sales)

$$\frac{76,660 \times 100}{500,607} = 15.3 \text{ per cent}$$

Capital turnover

$$\frac{500,607}{530,544} = 0.94 \text{ times}$$

Stocks
(at actual cost of finished goods)

$$\frac{115,321}{71,019} = 1.62 \text{ times}; \frac{12}{1.62} = 7.4 \text{ months}$$

Debtors

$$\frac{500,607}{105,001} = 4.77 \text{ times}; \frac{12}{4.77} = 2.5 \text{ months}$$

Fixed capital
(fixed assets)

$$\frac{500,607}{310,481} = 1.61 \text{ times}; \frac{12}{1.61} = 7.5 \text{ months}$$

# SOLUTIONS TO CHAPTER 11
## Administration

The ratio here will be 100:300 (or 1:3), see page 101.

# SOLUTIONS TO CHAPTER 12
## Solution 13
### Standard cost for one week of five days:

| | | |
|---|---|---|
| Labour | $8 \times £40 \times 5 =$ | £1,600 |
| Materials | $5 \times £15 \times 5 =$ | 375 |
| Overheads | $£60 \times 5 =$ | 300 |
| | | £2,275 |

### Actual cost for one week of five days:

| | | |
|---|---|---|
| Labour | $38 \times £41 =$ | £1,558 |
| Materials | $28 \times £14.50 =$ | 406 |
| Overheads | $=$ | 340 |
| | | £2,304 |

Total variance: £2,304 – £2,275 = £29 adverse.

This represents only 1 per cent of budget and would in practice probably not be investigated further, because of time constraints, but we will calculate the individual variances that go to make up the £29.

## Labour variances

| | |
|---|---|
| Standard cost | £1,600 |
| Actual cost | £1,558 |
| | £42 favourable |

This breaks down into labour rate variance and labour efficiency variance:

| | |
|---|---|
| Labour rate variance 38 hours (£40 – £41) | £38 adverse |
| Labour efficiency variance £40 (40 – 38) hours | £80 favourable |
| which nets back to the total labour variance: | £42 favourable |

## Material variances

| | |
|---|---|
| Standard cost | £375 |
| Actual cost | £406 |
| | £31 adverse |

This breaks down into material price variance and material usage variances:

| | |
|---|---|
| Material price variance 28 (£15 – £14.50) | £14 favourable |
| Material usage variance £15 (25 – 28) | £45 adverse |
| which nets back to the total materials variance: | £31 adverse |

## Overhead variance
This can be dealt with only in total:

| | |
|---|---|
| Standard cost | £300 |
| Actual cost | £340 |
| | £40 adverse |

Each of these variances should then be discussed in turn and suggestions made as to the most appropriate course of action.

# Solution 14

| | £ |
|---|---|
| Standard cost of a week for 20 delegates | |
| Delegates 20 × £7.20 × 40   = | 5,760.00 |
| Trainers 2 × £8.65 × 40   = | 692.00 |
| Overheads | 1,000.00 |
| | 7,452.00 |
| Actual cost of a week for 20 delegates | 7,810.80 |
| Adverse variance | 358.80 |

This variance represents 4.8 per cent of standard or accepted cost and may therefore be considered to be within accepted tolerances. However, let us undertake a further investigation. The variances will involve only labour and overheads as there are no materials that have been separately costed.

| | |
|---|---:|
| Actual cost of delegates | £5880 |
| Standard cost of delegates | £5760 |
| Adverse variance | £ 120 |

### Labour rate variance:

Actual hours × change in rate
$(20 \times 42) \times 20p$ =  168 favourable

### Labour efficiency variance:

Standard wage per hour × change in hours
$£7.20 \times [(42 - 40) \times 20]$  288.00 adverse

  20.00 adverse

| | |
|---|---:|
| Actual cost of trainers | 730.80 |
| Standard cost of trainers | 692.00 |
| Adverse variance | 38.80 |

### Labour rate variance:

$(2 \times 42) \times 5p$ =  4.20 adverse

### Labour efficiency variance:

$£8.65 \times [(42 - 40) \times 2]$ =  34.60 adverse

  38.80 adverse

### Overhead variance:

Standard overheads – Actual overhead
    1,000    –    1,200  =  200 adverse

### Total variance:

| | | |
|---|---|---:|
| Labour – Trainers | Adverse | 38.80 |
| Labour – Delegates | Adverse | 120.00 |
| Overheads | Adverse | 200.00 |
| | Adverse | 358.80 |

# Solution 15

Points that should be considered include:

- preparation of the planned or standard level of activity
- comparison of the actual activity with the planned activity
- significance of any variances (differences) obtained
- ascertaining the cause of the variance
- deciding on any necessary corrective action
- taking the necessary action quickly and effectively.

# SOLUTIONS TO CHAPTER 13
## Solution 16

If demand fell to 300 hours, the loss would be:

(333 hours − 300 hours) × 30 = £990

This is less than the loss involved in doing nothing, which would be £9,990. In the short run it is therefore better to keep going and look to save costs, increase prices or find new outlets.

## Solution 17

See the graph on the next page. The break even point is at 58 units sold.

Total revenue 70 × £25,000   =       £1,750,000
Total cost is £319,000 + (19500 × 70)  =  £1,684,000
Profit                                     £66,000

## Solution 18

1. Recruitment
2. Training
3. Establishing Departmental Contribution

## Solution 19

True cost of buying in                    £4,000
Add 25 per cent of £10,000                £2,500
                                          £6,500

Therefore the human resources department is cheaper, as the £10,000 head office costs have to be found, whether you buy in or not.

## Solution 19 continued

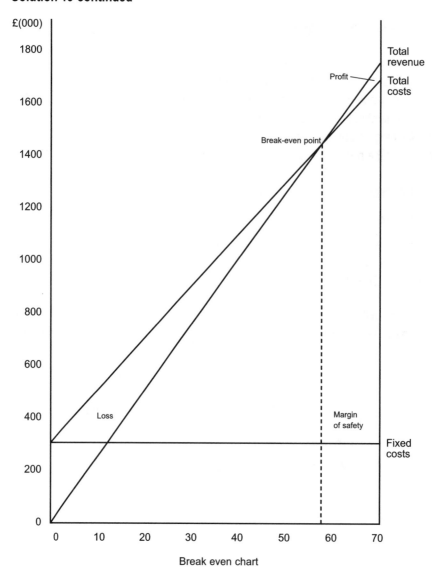

Break even chart

## Solution 20

1. Graph.
2. The contribution per hour is (£400 – £200)  =  £200.
3. The break even point is 150 hours.
4. The profit made is (300 units sold –150 units to break even) × £200 contribution per hour =  150 × £200  =  £30,000.
5. If sales fell to 100 hours we would be 50 hours below break even point. Each hour contributes £200 so the loss would be 50 × £200  =  £10,000.

# Solution 21

The total contribution at present is

300 hours × contribution per hour £200  =  £60,000

Under the new proposal the total contribution would be:

550 hours × contribution per hour £100  =  £55,000.

We would be losing £5,000 in contribution which would reduce the profit:

at present the profit is

contribution − fixed costs = £60,000 − £30,000  =  £30,000

under the new proposals the profit would be

£55,000 − £30,000 = £25,000

Therefore the change is not recommended unless it will lead to the introduction of a new clientele who will be of benefit to the organisation/department in the future.

# SOLUTIONS TO CHAPTER 15
## Solution 22a

Sales budget
Units sold

| Week | Plan | Actual | Cumulative | Actual |
|------|------|--------|------------|--------|
| 1 | 50 | | 50 | |
| 2 | 50 | | 100 | |
| 3 | 50 | | 150 | |
| 4 | 50 | | 200 | |
| 5 | 50 | | 250 | |
| 6 | 50 | | 300 | |
| 7 | 50 | | 350 | |
| 8 | 50 | | 400 | |
| 9 | 50 | | 450 | |
| 10 | 50 | | 500 | |
| 11 | 50 | | 550 | |
| 12 | 50 | | 600 | |

## Solution 22b

Materials budget

| Week | Opening balance | | Purchases | | | | Use | | | Closing balance | |
|------|------|------|------|------|------|------|------|------|------|------|------|
| | Plan | Actual | Plan | Cum. | Actual | Cum. | Plan | Cum. | Actual | Plan | Actual |
| 1 | | 10 | 25 | 25 | | | 25 | 25 | | 10 | |
| 2 | 10 | | 25 | 50 | | | 25 | 50 | | 10 | |
| 3 | 10 | | 25 | 75 | | | 25 | 75 | | 10 | |
| 4 | 10 | | 25 | 100 | | | 25 | 100 | | 10 | |
| 5 | 10 | | 25 | 125 | | | 25 | 125 | | 10 | |
| 6 | 10 | | 25 | 150 | | | 25 | 150 | | 10 | |
| 7 | 10 | | 25 | 175 | | | 25 | 175 | | 10 | |
| 8 | 10 | | 25 | 200 | | | 25 | 200 | | 10 | |
| 9 | 10 | | 25 | 225 | | | 25 | 225 | | 10 | |
| 10 | 10 | | 25 | 250 | | | 25 | 250 | | 10 | |
| 11 | 10 | | 25 | 275 | | | 25 | 275 | | 10 | |
| 12 | 10 | | 25 | 300 | | | 25 | 300 | | 10 | |

# Solution 22c

Labour budget

| Week | Planned hours | Actual hours | Planned hours | Actual hours |
|------|---------------|--------------|---------------|--------------|
| 1 | 30 | | 30 | |
| 2 | 30 | | 60 | |
| 3 | 30 | | 90 | |
| 4 | 30 | | 120 | |
| 5 | 30 | | 150 | |
| 6 | 30 | | 180 | |
| 7 | 30 | | 210 | |
| 8 | 30 | | 240 | |
| 9 | 30 | | 270 | |
| 10 | 30 | | 300 | |
| 11 | 30 | | 330 | |
| 12 | 30 | | 360 | |

# Solution 22d

Expenses budget

| Week | Planned (£) | Actual (£) | Cumulative Planned (£) | Actual (£) |
|------|-------------|------------|------------------------|------------|
| 1 | 40 | | 40 | |
| 2 | 40 | | 80 | |
| 3 | 40 | | 120 | |
| 4 | 40 | | 160 | |
| 5 | 40 | | 200 | |
| 6 | 40 | | 240 | |
| 7 | 40 | | 280 | |
| 8 | 40 | | 320 | |
| 9 | 40 | | 360 | |
| 10 | 40 | | 400 | |
| 11 | 40 | | 440 | |
| 12 | 40 | | 480 | |

## Solution 22e

Cash budget

| Week | 1 | 2 | 3 | 4 | 5 | 6 | 7 | 8 | 9 | 10 | 11 | 12 |
|---|---|---|---|---|---|---|---|---|---|---|---|---|
| Opening balance | £400 | (£105) | (£610) | (£1,115) | ((£1,620) | (£1,125) | (£630) | (£135) | £360 | £855 | £1,350 | £1,845 |
| Add sales receipt | | | | | 1,000 | 1,000 | 1,000 | 1,000 | 1,000 | 1,000 | 1,000 | 1,000 |
| Balance | 400 | (105) | (610) | (1,115) | (620) | (125) | 370 | 865 | 1,360 | 1,855 | 2,350 | 2,845 |
| Deduct Payments: | | | | | | | | | | | | |
| Labour | 450 | 450 | 450 | 450 | 450 | 450 | 450 | 450 | 450 | 450 | 450 | 450 |
| Materials | 15 | 15 | 15 | 15 | 15 | 15 | 15 | 15 | 15 | 15 | 15 | 15 |
| Expenses | 40 | 40 | 40 | 40 | 40 | 40 | 40 | 40 | 40 | 40 | 40 | 40 |
| Total | £505 | £505 | £505 | £505 | £505 | £505 | £505 | £505 | £505 | £505 | £505 | £505 |
| Balance c/f | (105) | (610) | (1,115) | (1,620) | (1,125) | (630) | (135) | 360 | 855 | 1,350 | 1,845 | 2,340 |

The cash budget clearly shows a cash-flow deficit for the first seven weeks, rising to a maximum of £1,620 in week 4. This might necessitate a change in the plan or it might be possible to obtain an overdraft facility of £2,000 for 10 weeks from the bank. This will allow some flexibility if the plan has any errors in it.

# Solution 22f

### Forecast profit and loss account for three months

| | £ | £ |
|---|---|---|
| Sales | | 12,000 |
| Less Cost of sales: | | |
| Opening inventory | 6 | |
| Add material purchased | 180 | |
| | 186 | |
| Less closing inventory | 6 | 180 |
| | | |
| Gross profit | | 11,820 |
| Less expenses: | | |
| Wages | 5,400 | |
| Expenses | 480 | 5,880 |
| | | |
| Net profit | | 5,940 |

# Solution 22g

### Balance sheet as at the end of three months

| | £ | | £ |
|---|---|---|---|
| Inventory | 6 | Capital | 406 |
| Debtors | 4,000 | Profit | 5,940 |
| Bank | 2,340 | | |
| | 6,346 | | 6,346 |

# Solution 23

| | Flexed budget £ | Actual costs £ | Variance favourable/ (adverse)[4] £ |
|---|---|---|---|
| Direct materials[1] | 120,000 | 122,000 | (2,000) |
| Direct labour[1] | 240,000 | 236,000 | 4,000 |
| Variable overhead | 24,000 | 28,000 | (4,000) |
| Total variable costs | 384,000 | 386,000 | (2,000) |
| Fixed overhead[2] | 80,000 | 84,000 | (4,000) |
| Total costs[3] | 464,000 | 470,000 | (6,000) |

Notes:

1. The budgeted variable costs have been flexed by 20 per cent because the actual activity was 60 per cent compared with a budgeted level of 50 per cent.
2. The fixed costs have not been changed because they should not alter with activity.
3. The total flexed budget costs of £464,00 are compared with the total actual cost of £470,000.
4. The terms favourable or adverse relate to impact on profit.

# Solution 24

### Cash budget for Personnel Ltd
### for the six months ended 30th June 2005

|  | Jan £'000 | Feb £'000 | March £'000 | April £'000 | May £'000 | June £'000 | Total £'000 |
|---|---|---|---|---|---|---|---|
| Receipts | 240 | 1,200 | 1,600 | 800 | 1,400 | 1,800 | 7,040 |
| Payments: |  |  |  |  |  |  |  |
| Materials | 100 | 400 | 600 | 400 | 1,000 | 200 | 2,700 |
| Wages | 440 | 480 | 500 | 500 | 550 | 580 | 3,050 |
| Overhead expenses | 60 | 50 | 50 | 60 | 70 | 80 | 370 |
|  | 600 | 930 | 1,150 | 960 | 1,620 | 860 | 6,120 |
| Net receipts | (360) | 270 | 450 | (160) | (220) | 940 | 920 |
| Opening balance | 100 | (260) | 10 | 460 | 300 | 80 | 100 |
| Closing balance | (260) | 10 | 460 | 300 | 80 | 1,020 | 1,020 |

Note:
The opening balance in the total column is the balance at the beginning of the year and not the total of the row, whilst the closing balance is the balance at the end of the year.

# SOLUTIONS TO CHAPTER 16
## Solution 25

Cash budget

| | January | February | March | April | May | June |
|---|---|---|---|---|---|---|
| Opening balance in hand | £2,000 | | | | £506 | £3,182 |
| (overdrawn) | | (£964) | (£3,082) | (£2,170) | | |
| Add receipts from sales | | 846 | 5,076 | 5,640 | 5,640 | 5,640 |
| Total | £2,000 | (£118) | £1,994 | £3,470 | £6,146 | £8,822 |
| *Less payments:* | | | | | | |
| Brown | 800 | 800 | 800 | 800 | 800 | 800 |
| Wood | 1,200 | 1,200 | 1,200 | 1,200 | 1,200 | 1,200 |
| Rent | 40 | 40 | 40 | 40 | 40 | 40 |
| Postage | 924 | 924 | 924 | 924 | 924 | 924 |
| Rates, etc. | | | 1,200 | | | 1,200 |
| Equipment | | | | | | 5,000 |
| Total | £2,964 | £2,964 | £4,164 | £2,964 | £2,964 | £9,164 |
| Balance c/f in hand | | | | 506 | 3,182 | |
| (overdrawn) | (964) | (3,082) | (2,170) | | | (342) |

If the forecasts are correct and Brown can obtain an overdraft facility of £4,000 for six months, the business seems likely to be successful. It should be borne in mind, however, that in order to produce 10 models he will have to work 80 hours a week and may find that impossible to achieve over a long period of time.

# Solution 26

| | July | August | September | October | November | December |
|---|---|---|---|---|---|---|
| | £ | £ | £ | £ | £ | £ |
| Opening balance | 3,000 | 2,380 | 4,760 | (10,660) | (4,600) | 4,260 |
| Sales receipts | 9,600 | 11,200 | 12,800 | 14,400 | 15,200 | 10,400 |
| TOTAL CASH AVAILABLE | 12,600 | 13,580 | 17,560 | 3,740 | 10,600 | 14,660 |
| Payments: | | | | | | |
| Labour | 4,000 | 2,600 | 2,200 | 2,000 | 1,800 | 1,400 |
| Materials | 3,600 | 4,080 | 4,320 | 4,800 | 3,120 | 2,640 |
| Variable expenses | 720 | 800 | 520 | 440 | 400 | 360 |
| | 1,600 | 1,040 | 880 | 800 | 720 | 560 |
| Fixed expenses | 300 | 300 | 300 | 300 | 300 | 300 |
| Capital expenditure | – | – | 20,000 | – | – | – |
| TOTAL PAYMENTS | 10,220 | 8,820 | 28,220 | 8,340 | 6,340 | 5,260 |
| TOTAL CASH – TOTAL PAYMENTS | | | | | | |
| Balance carried f/wrd | 2,380 | 4,760 | (10,660) | (4,600) | 4,260 | 9,400 |

# Solution 27

|  | November | December | January | February | March | April |
|---|---|---|---|---|---|---|
|  | £ | £ | £ | £ | £ | £ |
| Opening balance | (1,050) | (2,100) | (500) | (1,575) | 6,575 | 350 |
| Cash receipts | 5,400 | 9,000 | 6,300 | 20,700 | 3,600 | 7,200 |
| Received from debtors | 800 | 600 | 1,000 | 700 | 2,300 | 400 |
| TOTAL CASH AVAILABLE | 5,150 | 7,150 | 6,800 | 19,825 | 12,475 | 7,950 |
| Cash purchases | 2,250 | 3,750 | 2,625 | 8,625 | 1,500 | 3,000 |
| Previous credit purchases | 3,000 | 2,250 | 3,750 | 2,625 | 8,625 | 1,500 |
| Wages | 2,000 | 2,000 | 2,000 | 2,000 | 2,000 | 2,000 |
|  | 7,250 | 8,000 | 8,375 | 13,250 | 12,125 | 6,500 |
| Balance carried f/wrd | (2,100) | (500) | (1,575) | 6,575 | 350 | 1,450 |

Notes:

1. The opening balance of (£1,050) overdrawn comes from the overdraft shown on the opening balance sheet.
2. Cash receipts are obtained by taking 90 per cent of November sales of £6,000, which gives £5,400. The other 10 per cent is shown as receipts from debtors, £600, in December.
3. Receipts from debtors, £800, comes from the debtors shown in the opening balance sheet.
4. Cash payments, £2,250, is derived from the fact that the gross profit margin is 25 per cent of the selling price, which is 25 per cent of £6,000 (= £1,500). This means that the cost of sales, ie purchases, is £4,500. As 50 per cent of the purchases is paid for straight away and 50 per cent in the next month, £2,250 is therefore cash purchases this month (November), and £2,250 previous cash purchases next month (December).
5. The previous credit purchases for November, £3,000, comes from the creditors in the opening balance sheet.

NB The processes detailed above are followed each month through to June.

# SOLUTIONS TO CHAPTER 17
## Solution 28
### *Pay-back*

| | | |
|---|---|---|
| Cost of new machine | | £80,000 |
| Annual savings | £ 14,000 pa | |
| Pay-back | $\dfrac{£\,80,000}{£\,14,000}$ = | 5.7 years |

If Green is looking for a three-year pay-back, the scheme would be rejected. The decision would be reversed, however, if he required a six-year pay-back.

### *Rate of return*

| | | |
|---|---|---|
| Cost of new machine | | 80,000 |
| Average annual savings | £14,000 | |

As the same sum of money is saved each year the average annual saving is the same as the annual saving.

| | | |
|---|---|---|
| Rate of return: | $\dfrac{£14,000 \times 100}{£80,000}$ = | 17.5% |

If Green requires a 15 per cent rate of return this scheme could go forward.

### *Discounted cash flow*

| | £ | £ | £ |
|---|---|---|---|
| Cost of new machine | | | 80,000 |
| Savings: | | | |
| 1. | $14,000 \times 0.8696$ = | 12,174.4 | |
| 2. | $14,000 \times 0.7561$ = | 10,585.4 | |
| 3. | $14,000 \times 0.6575$ = | 9,205.0 | |
| 4. | $14,000 \times 0.5718$ = | 8,005.2 | |
| 5. | $14,000 \times 0.4972$ = | 6,960.8 | |
| 6. | $14,000 \times 0.4323$ = | 6,052.2 | |
| 7. | $14,000 \times 0.3759$ = | 5,262.6 | |
| 8. | $14,000 \times 0.3269$ = | 4,576.6 | |

| | |
|---|---|
| Present value of future cash flows | 62,822.2 |
| Net present value of scheme | – 17,177.8 |

The scheme would be rejected on this criterion, as it would not make the 15 per cent required, but there may be criteria other than the financial one that could make Green decide to go ahead anyway, for example his competitive position.

In using the discounted cash flow (DCF) approach, it is possible to take a short cut when the same sum of money is involved each year. So far we have used the 'present value of £1' column but we could use the 'Present value of £1 received at end of period' column, when we have:

| | | |
|---|---|---|
| Cost of new machine | | £80,000 |
| Savings | £14,000 × 4.4873 | |
| Present value of future cash flows | | £62,822.2 |
| Net present value of the scheme | | £– 17,177.8 |

It should be emphasised that this approach can be employed only when the same sum of money is involved each year.

## Solution 29
### Pay-back

| | | |
|---|---|---|
| Cost of insulation | | £130,000 |
| Savings | £ 16,000 pa | |
| Pay-back | $\dfrac{£130,000}{£16,000}$ = | 8.1 years |

If the authority requires a pay-back of five years this scheme would be rejected, but if the criterion was 10 years it could go forward.

### Rate of return

| | | |
|---|---|---|
| Cost of insulation | | £130,000 |
| Average annual savings | | £ 16,000 |
| Rate of return: | $\dfrac{£16,000 \times 100}{£130,000}$ = | 12.3% |

If a return of 8 per cent is required this scheme could proceed, but 14 per cent would cause it to be rejected.

### Discounted cash flow

| | | |
|---|---|---|
| Cost of insulation | | £130,000 |
| Savings: | £16,000 × 8.5595 | |
| Present value of future cash flows | | £136,952 |
| Net present value of the scheme | | + £ 6,952 |

The scheme would be accepted, as it would make more than the 8 percent required.

## Solution 30

| Year | £ | | £ |
|------|------|---|------|
| 1. | 1,000 × 0.9259 | = | 925.9 |
| 2. | 2,000 × 0.8573 | = | 1,714.6 |
| 3. | 4,000 × 0.7938 | = | 3,175.2 |
| 4. | 2,000 × 0.7350 | = | 1,470.0 |
| 5. | 1,000 × 0.6806 | = | 680.6 |
| | Total | | 7,966.3 |

The costs of £8,000 are not recovered, so purely on the basis of the numbers the machine would not be purchased. However this is a marginal decision as the difference is only £33.70 and the human resources manager would be able to make a strong case for the scheme to proceed. Particularly when you remember that the cash savings are estimates. The £33.70 represents the net present value of the scheme and it is negative because the present value of the future cash flows £7,966.30 is less than the outlay of £8,000.

## Solution 31

| | £ |
|------|------|
| Outlay now | 40,000 |
| Income £10,000 pa for five years @ 8 per cent | |
| £10,000 × 3.9927   = | 39,927 |
| Net present value of the scheme   = | −     73 |

The scheme is not quite making the 8 per cent return that is required, but it is so close that the decision will be made on the basis of convincing argument rather than the numbers, which are not conclusive.

# Appendix

# Discounted cash flow: selected tables

Only those sections of a full set of tables that relate to Chapter 6 are shown here.

## 8 per cent of return

| Year | Amount to which £1 will accumulate | Present value of £1 | Present value of £1 received at end of period | Present value of £1 received continuously | Amount received at end of year which will recover initial investment of £1 | Amount received continuously which will recover initial investment of £1 | Year |
|---|---|---|---|---|---|---|---|
| 1 | 1.0800 | 0.9259 | 0.9259 | 0.9625 | 1.0800 | 1.0390 | 1 |
| 2 | 1.1664 | 0.8573 | 1.7833 | 1.8537 | 0.5608 | 0.5395 | 2 |
| 3 | 1.2597 | 0.7938 | 2.5771 | 2.6789 | 0.3880 | 0.3733 | 3 |
| 4 | 1.3605 | 0.7350 | 3.3121 | 3.4429 | 0.3019 | 0.2905 | 4 |
| 5 | 1.4693 | 0.6806 | 3.9927 | 4.1504 | 0.2505 | 0.2409 | 5 |
| 6 | 1.5869 | 0.6302 | 4.6229 | 4.8054 | 0.2163 | 0.2081 | 6 |
| 7 | 1.7138 | 0.5835 | 5.2064 | 5.4120 | 0.1921 | 0.1848 | 7 |
| 8 | 1.8509 | 0.5403 | 5.7466 | 5.9736 | 0.1740 | 0.1674 | 8 |
| 9 | 1.9990 | 0.5002 | 6.2469 | 6.4936 | 0.1601 | 0.1540 | 9 |
| 10 | 2.1589 | 0.4632 | 6.7101 | 6.9750 | 0.1490 | 0.1434 | 10 |
| 11 | 2.3316 | 0.4289 | 7.1390 | 7.4209 | 0.1401 | 0.1348 | 11 |
| 12 | 2.6182 | 0.3971 | 7.5361 | 7.8337 | 0.1327 | 0.1277 | 12 |
| 13 | 2.7196 | 0.3677 | 7.9038 | 8.2159 | 0.1265 | 0.1217 | 13 |
| 14 | 2.9372 | 0.3405 | 8.2442 | 8.5698 | 0.1213 | 0.1167 | 14 |
| 15 | 3.1722 | 0.3152 | 8.5595 | 8.8975 | 0.1168 | 0.1124 | 15 |
| 16 | 3.4259 | 0.2919 | 8.8514 | 9.2009 | 0.1150 | 0.1087 | 16 |
| 17 | 3.7000 | 0.2703 | 9.1216 | 9.4818 | 0.1096 | 1.1055 | 17 |
| 18 | 3.9960 | 0.2502 | 9.3719 | 9.7420 | 0.1067 | 1.1026 | 18 |
| 19 | 4.3157 | 0.2317 | 9.6036 | 9.9828 | 0.1041 | 0.1002 | 19 |
| 20 | 4.6610 | 0.2145 | 9.8181 | 10.2058 | 0.1019 | 0.0980 | 20 |
| 21 | 5.0338 | 0.1987 | 10.0168 | 10.4123 | 0.0998 | 0.0960 | 21 |
| 22 | 5.4365 | 0.1839 | 10.2007 | 10.6035 | 0.0980 | 0.0943 | 22 |
| 23 | 5.8715 | 0.1703 | 10.3711 | 10.7806 | 0.0964 | 0.0928 | 23 |
| 24 | 6.3412 | 0.1577 | 10.5288 | 10.9445 | 0.0950 | 0.0914 | 24 |
| 25 | 6.8485 | 0.1460 | 10.6748 | 11.0963 | 0.0937 | 0.0901 | 25 |

## 15 per cent of return

| Year | Amount to which £1 will accumulate | Present value of £1 | Present value of £1 received at end of period | Present value of £1 received continuously | Amount received at end of year which will recover initial investment of £1 | Amount received continuously which will recover initial investment of £1 | Year |
|---|---|---|---|---|---|---|---|
| 1 | 1.1500 | 0.8696 | 0.8696 | 0.9333 | 1.1500 | 1.0715 | 1 |
| 2 | 1.3225 | 0.7561 | 1.6257 | 1.7448 | 0.6151 | 0.5731 | 2 |
| 3 | 1.5209 | 0.6575 | 2.2832 | 2.4505 | 0.4380 | 0.4081 | 3 |
| 4 | 1.7490 | 0.5718 | 2.8550 | 3.0641 | 0.3503 | 0.3264 | 4 |
| 5 | 2.0114 | 0.4972 | 3.3522 | 3.5977 | 0.2983 | 0.2780 | 5 |
| 6 | 2.3131 | 0.4323 | 3.7845 | 4.0617 | 0.2642 | 0.2462 | 6 |
| 7 | 2.6600 | 0.3759 | 4.1604 | 4.4652 | 0.2404 | 0.2240 | 7 |
| 8 | 3.0590 | 0.3269 | 4.4873 | 4.8160 | 0.2229 | 0.2076 | 8 |
| 9 | 3.5179 | 0.2843 | 4.7716 | 5.1211 | 0.2096 | 0.1953 | 9 |
| 10 | 4.0456 | 0.2472 | 5.0188 | 5.3864 | 0.1993 | 0.1857 | 10 |
| 11 | 4.6524 | 0.2149 | 5.2337 | 5.6171 | 0.1911 | 0.1780 | 11 |
| 12 | 5.3503 | 0.1869 | 5.4206 | 5.8177 | 0.1845 | 0.1719 | 12 |
| 13 | 6.1528 | 0.1625 | 5.5831 | 5.9921 | 0.1791 | 0.1669 | 13 |
| 14 | 7.0757 | 0.1413 | 5.7245 | 6.1438 | 0.1747 | 0.1628 | 14 |
| 15 | 8.1371 | 0.1229 | 5.8474 | 6.2757 | 0.1710 | 0.1593 | 15 |
| 16 | 9.3576 | 0.1069 | 5.9542 | 6.3904 | 0.1679 | 0.1565 | 16 |
| 17 | 10.7613 | 0.0929 | 6.0472 | 6.4901 | 0.1654 | 0.1541 | 17 |
| 18 | 12.3755 | 0.0808 | 6.1280 | 6.5769 | 0.1632 | 0.1520 | 18 |
| 19 | 14.2318 | 0.0703 | 6.1982 | 6.6523 | 0.1613 | 0.1503 | 19 |
| 20 | 16.3665 | 0.0611 | 6.2593 | 6.7178 | 0.1598 | 0.1489 | 20 |
| 21 | 18.8215 | 0.0531 | 6.3125 | 6.7749 | 0.1584 | 0.1476 | 21 |
| 22 | 21.6447 | 0.0462 | 6.3587 | 6.8245 | 0.1573 | 0.1465 | 22 |
| 23 | 24.8915 | 0.0402 | 6.3988 | 6.8676 | 0.1563 | 0.1456 | 23 |
| 24 | 28.6252 | 0.0349 | 6.4338 | 6.9051 | 0.1554 | 0.1448 | 24 |
| 25 | 32.9190 | 0.0304 | 6.4641 | 6.9377 | 0.1547 | 0.1441 | 25 |

**16 per cent of return**

| Year | Amount to which £1 will accumulate | Present value of £1 | Present value of £1 received at end of period | Present value of £1 received continuously | Amount received at end of year which will recover initial investment of £1 | Amount received continuously which will recover initial investment of £1 | Year |
|---|---|---|---|---|---|---|---|
| 1 | 1.1600 | 0.8621 | 0.8621 | 0.9293 | 1.1600 | 1.0760 | 1 |
| 2 | 1.3456 | 0.7432 | 1.6052 | 1.7305 | 0.6230 | 0.5779 | 2 |
| 3 | 1.5609 | 0.6407 | 2.2459 | 2.4211 | 0.4453 | 0.4130 | 3 |
| 4 | 1.8106 | 0.5523 | 2.7982 | 3.0165 | 0.3574 | 0.3315 | 4 |
| 5 | 2.1003 | 0.4761 | 3.2743 | 3.5298 | 0.3054 | 0.2833 | 5 |
| 6 | 2.4364 | 0.4104 | 3.6847 | 3.9722 | 0.2714 | 0.2517 | 6 |
| 7 | 2.8262 | 0.3538 | 4.0386 | 4.3537 | 0.2476 | 0.2297 | 7 |
| 8 | 3.2784 | 0.3050 | 4.3436 | 4.6825 | 0.2302 | 0.2136 | 8 |
| 9 | 3.8030 | 0.2630 | 4.6065 | 4.9660 | 0.2171 | 0.2014 | 9 |
| 10 | 4.4114 | 0.2267 | 4.8332 | 5.2103 | 0.2069 | 0.1919 | 10 |
| 11 | 5.1173 | 0.1954 | 5.0286 | 5.4210 | 0.1989 | 0.1845 | 11 |
| 12 | 5.9360 | 0.1685 | 5.1971 | 5.6026 | 0.1924 | 0.1785 | 12 |
| 13 | 6.8858 | 0.1452 | 5.3423 | 5.7592 | 0.1872 | 0.1736 | 13 |
| 14 | 7.9875 | 0.1252 | 5.4675 | 5.8941 | 0.1829 | 0.1697 | 14 |
| 15 | 9.2655 | 0.1079 | 5.5755 | 6.0105 | 0.1794 | 0.1664 | 15 |
| 16 | 10.7480 | 0.0930 | 5.6685 | 6.1108 | 0.1764 | 0.1636 | 16 |
| 17 | 12.4677 | 0.0802 | 5.7487 | 6.1972 | 0.1740 | 0.1614 | 17 |
| 18 | 14.4625 | 0.0691 | 5.8178 | 6.2718 | 0.1719 | 0.1594 | 18 |
| 19 | 16.7765 | 0.0596 | 5.8775 | 6.3360 | 0.1701 | 0.1578 | 19 |
| 20 | 19.4608 | 0.0514 | 5.9288 | 6.3914 | 0.1687 | 0.1565 | 20 |
| 21 | 22.5745 | 0.0443 | 5.9731 | 6.4392 | 0.1674 | 0.1553 | 21 |
| 22 | 26.1864 | 0.0382 | 6.0113 | 6.4803 | 0.1664 | 0.1543 | 22 |
| 23 | 30.3762 | 0.0329 | 6.0442 | 6.5158 | 0.1654 | 0.1535 | 23 |
| 24 | 35.2364 | 0.0284 | 6.0726 | 6.5464 | 0.1647 | 0.1528 | 24 |
| 25 | 40.8742 | 0.0245 | 6.0971 | 6.5728 | 0.1640 | 0.1521 | 25 |

# Glossary

**ABC** or **Activity based costing**   This method of costing apportions overheads according to the use each support service makes of each activity *ie it uses cost drivers*.

**Absorption costing**   This method of costing which is also known as *total costing* helps to ensure that organisational costs are fully recovered.

**Accounting period**   Normally 12 months as far as the financial accounts are concerned, to coincide with the tax year. So far as the management accounts are concerned, it can be any period ranging from one week to one year. It is generally thought necessary to provide management information at least once every four weeks.

**Accounting principles**   A set of rules that have to be followed to ensure that financial information is prepared on a consistent basis from year to year.

**Accounting rate of return**   The average annual cash-flow generated by a scheme expressed as a percentage of the outlay.

**Acid test**   Test of the ability of an organisation to pay its way in the short term, up to four months, given by the ratio of quick assets to current liabilities.

**Added value**   The value an organisation adds to bought-in goods and services. It goes to meet wages and then profits.

**Articles of association**   Internal rules that state the rights and duties of directors and shareholders of a company.

**Assets**   Items belonging to the organisation that have either a long-term or a short-term value. Those having a long-term value are items like machinery and plant. They are called fixed assets.

**Authorised capital**   The total amount of money that the organisation is authorised to raise by the issue of share capital. The authorised capital is subject to stamp duty, and so organisations do not state high authorised capital figures when they are first formed. The authorised share capital is not set for all time, and can be varied if necessary.

**Balance sheet**   A statement of the financial position of an organisation at a date.

**Behavioural impact**   The impact of the budgetary process on the people working in an organisation.

**Book value** The value at which an asset is shown in the balance sheet.

**Break even** The point at which total costs are equal to total revenues.

**Budget** A budget is a forecast or estimate of events over a stated future interval of time, eg one year, five years or six months.

**Capital employed (1)** The total of the assets owned. The net capital employed is more usually used in calculating ratios and is the total assets less the current liabilities.

**Capital employed (2)** All the resources employed. The total of the liabilities of an organisation.

**Capital items** Items that last for several years. Examples are machinery used in manufacture, motor vehicles, land and buildings.

**Cost-benefit analysis** A system of measuring the costs and benefits of a capital scheme that includes the social costs and benefits.

**Credit terms** Providing or receiving goods or services for which payment will be made at a later date.

**Creditors** People or organisations that are owed money by an undertaking.

**Current assets** Assets that are normally used up in one financial period and change from day to day. Examples are stock, debtors and cash.

**Current liabilities** Liabilities that must be settled within a short time; they fluctuate from day to day. Examples are creditors and bank overdrafts.

**Current ratio** Measure of the organisation's ability to pay its way in the period between about three and nine months in the future. Given by the ratio of current assets to current liabilities.

**Debenture** A certificate issued by a company acknowledging a debt.

**Debtors** People or organisations that owe money to an undertaking.

**Depreciation** Method of allocating the cost of a fixed asset over its useful life.

**Direct expenses** Those expenses that are directly attributable to the product or service provided.

**Discounted cash flow (DCF)** Future cash flows discounted to give their present value.

**Dividend** Distribution of profits to the shareholders. Usually expressed as a dividend of $x$ p in the £ on the nominal value of shares. Generally paid twice a year in the form of the interim and final dividends.

**Earnings** Money received or due for goods or services provided by the organisation.

**Equity** The equity of the business is the part that belongs to the owners. It is what remains after all outside interests have received their money.

**Expenses** Money paid or due to be paid by the organisation for revenue, goods or services it has received.

**Fixed assets** Assets held for many years to earn profits. Examples are land and buildings, or plant and machinery.

**Fixed overheads** Expenses that do not vary with the level of activity.

**Gearing** Relationship between the share capital and loan capital of a business.

**Goodwill** The excess over the book value of a business that is received when the business is sold.

**Historical cost** The cost at which the assets were obtained.

**Income statement** Used to calculate the profit or loss of an organisation in an accounting period. Made up of: (1) The *manufacturing account*, showing the costs of goods made; (2) The *trading account*, showing the gross profit or loss; the difference between the cost price and selling price of the goods; (3) The *profit and loss account*, showing the net profit or loss.

**Inventory** Stock.

**Issued capital** The shares that have been issued by the organisation in order to raise money. It is issued in return for cash.

**Job cost** Cost of a single job or operation.

**Liabilities** Money that the organisation owes.

**Limited company** A company which does not offer its shares to the general public.

**Long-term liabilities** Long-term debts.

**Manufacturing account** A financial statement showing the cost of the goods that have been made by a company.

**Margin of safety**  The excess of sales over the break even point.

**Marginal cost**  The cost of one more unit.

**Memorandum of association** Constitution of the company.

**Net assets**  Total assets less current liabilities.

**Net capital employed (NCE)**  The resources that are employed in the business for more than one year; enables the return on the long-term investment to be found. The net capital employed is calculated by deducting the current liabilities from the total assets.

**NPV**  Net present value of a scheme.

**Ordinary shares**  Share capital that has voting rights and receives its dividends at the discretion of the directors of the company.

**Payback**  The time it takes to recover the outlay on a scheme from the funds generated by the scheme.

**Preference shares**  Share capital that has a fixed rate of dividend, and receives its dividends before the rest of the share capital.

**Prime costs**  Direct materials, direct labour and direct expenses added together.

**Profit**  Surplus of earnings over expenses.

**Profit and loss account**  A financial statement that shows the profit an organisation has made or the loss it has incurred. Some times referred to as the revenue account.

**Public limited company (PLC)**   Limited company that conforms to European Community regulations.

**PV**  Present value of the future cash flows discounted at the appropriate rate.

**Quick assets**  Those that are quickly and easily realisable – normally debtors and cash.

**Quick ratio**  Acid test.

**Reserves**  Profits that are retained in the business – rarely cash.

**Retained profits**  Reserves.

**Revenue account**  See *profit and loss account*.

**Revenue items**  Items that are completely used up or discharged in one year. Examples are salaries, wages, heating, raw materials.

**Revenue reserves**  Distributable to shareholders.

**Share capital**  The amount received from the shareholders of the business.

**Share premium**  A capital reserve (one which cannot be distributed to the shareholders) created when the company sells its shares at a price in excess of the nominal value.

**Sole trader**  An organisation consisting of a single individual who takes full responsibility for the work undertaken.

**Standard cost**  Predetermined or expected cost.

**Stock turnover**  Number of times the stock is turned over in a financial period, given by the ratio of cost of goods sold to cost of stock.

**Sustainable Development**  The issue of taking environmental and social concerns into account when making business and political decisions in order to ensure a better quality of life for everyone.

**Turnover**  Total sales value.

**Variable overheads**  Indirect expenses that vary with the level of activity.

**Variances**  Differences between standard and actual performance. Can be either favourable or adverse.

**Working capital**  Capital needed to keep the business operating until more money is obtained from operations. It is current assets minus current liabilities.

**Working capital ratio**  The ratio of current assets to current liabilities.

**Z Score**  This approach attempts to identify key ratios that enable organisational performance to be analysed in order to predict those organisations that are in danger of failing.

# Bibliography

ATKINSON, A., KAPLAN, R. and YOUNG, S. (2004) *Management accounting*. 4th ed. Hertfordshire: Prentice Hall.

ATTRILL, P. and McLANEY, A. (2004) *Accounting and finance for non specialists*. 4th ed. Hertfordshire: FT/Prentice Hall.

BODNOR, G. and HOPWOOD, W. (2004) *Accounting information systems*. 9th ed. Hertfordshire: Prentice Hall.

DAVIES, D.B. (1997) *The art of managing finance*. 3rd ed. London: McGraw-Hill.

DRURY, C. (2004) *Management and cost accounting*. 6th ed. London: International Thompson Business Press.

DYSON, J.R. (2004) *Accounting for non-accounting students*. 6th ed. Singapore: Pitman/FT.

FAIR, H. (1992) *Personnel and profit: the payoff from people*. Trowbridge: IPM.

GARRISON, N. and SEAL. W. (2003) *Management accounting*. Maidenhead: McGraw-Hill.

HENLEY, D., HOLTHAM C.W. and PERRIN J.R. (1992) *Public sector accounting and financial control*. 4th ed. London: Chapman and Hall.

*Key British enterprises* (annual edition) (2003) London: Dunn and Bradstreet.

McLANEY, E. and ATTRILL, P. (1999) *Accounting: an introduction*. Hertfordshire: Prentice Hall.

MONCARZ, E. (2004) *Accounting for the hospitality industry*. Hertfordshire: Prentice Hall.

PIZZEY, A. (1998) *Finance and accounting*. London: Pitman.

WERNER, M.L., and JONES, K.H. (2004) *Introduction to accounting, (combined)*. Hertfordshire: Prentice Hall.

YOUNG, S. M., (2003) *Techniques of management accounting: an essential guide for managers and financial professionals.* Maidenhead: McGraw-Hill.

YOUNG, S. M. (2004) *Readings in management accounting.* 4th ed. Hertfordshire: Prentice Hall.

# Management Standards

2.     **Managing Finance**

   2.1     **Performance Infrastructure**

   **Operational indicators**

   Practitioners must be able to:

   1. Manage financial resources to achieve goals and objectives through the budgetary planning and control process

   2. Interpret information from key financial statements.

   **Knowledge indicators**

   Practitioners must be able to understand, explain and critically evaluate:

   1. Financial statements and their meaning

   2. The budgetary process

   3. Flow of money in a business.

   **Indicative content**

   1. Structure, content and interpretation of simple balance sheets, profit & loss accounts and trading statements

   2. Ratio analysis – definition and interpretation

   3. Basic costing concepts & techniques: analysis of costs, marginal costing, standard costing

   4. Cash flow and Cash budgets

   5. Budgetary planning and control.

## 2.2 Performance Differentiators

### Operational indicators

Practitioners must be able to:

1. Evaluate business plans for functional organisational projects

2. Critically appraise proposals for capital projects

3. Analyse financial and other information used in making outsourcing decisions

4. Evaluate the financial implications of sustainable development.

### Knowledge indicators

Practitioners must be able to understand, explain and critically evaluate:

1. The business planning process

2. Capital budgets and Project appraisal

3. Outsourcing – the make or buy decision

4. Concepts of sustainable development.

### Indicative content

1. Structure and content of business plans

2. Project appraisal: discounted cash flow (net present value), accounting rate of return, pay-back, cost-benefit analysis

3. Marginal costing

4. Financial aspects of sustainability in relation to resource management.

# Professional Standards Index

This index cross-references to chapters in the text the main subject areas as set out in the Professional Standards of the Institute of Personnel and Development for Managing Financial Information.

| UNIT | INDEX OF COMPETENCES | CHAPTERS |
|------|----------------------|----------|
| **B3** | **Manage the use of financial resources** | |
| Element B.3.1 | Make recommendations for expenditure | 12, 16, 17 |
| Element B.3.2 | Control expenditure against budgets | 3, 7, 9, 11, 13, 14, 15 |
| **B5** | **Secure financial resources for your organisation's plans** | |
| Element B.5.1 | Review the generation and allocation of financial resources | 4, 5, 6, 8, 9, 10, 14, 15 |
| Element B.5.2 | Evaluate proposals for expenditure | 3, 7, 12, 16, 17 |
| Element B.5.3 | Obtain financial resources for your organisation's activities | 8, 13, 14, 17 |

# Index